ALWAYS PLENTY TO DO

GROWING UP ON A FARM IN THE LONG AGO

PAMELA RINEY-KEHRBERG

A WINDWORD BOOK FOR YOUNG READERS

TEXAS TECH UNIVERSITY PRESS

This book is typeset in Amasis. The paper used in this book meets the minimum requirements of ANSI/NISO Z39.48-1992 (R1997). ∞

Designed by Kasey McBeath

Library of Congress Cataloging-in-Publication Data
Riney-Kehrberg, Pamela.
Always plenty to do : growing up on a farm in the long ago / Pamela Riney-Kehrberg.
p. cm.
Summary: "The story of childhood on America's farms in the late nineteenth and early twentieth century; reveals what farm children saw, heard, smelled, tasted, and felt—and how they worked, played, and learned. Includes historical photographs" —Provided by publisher.
Includes bibliographical references and index.
ISBN 978-0-89672-692-5 (hardcover (litho case) : alk. paper)
1. Farm life—United States—History—Juvenile literature. 2. Rural children—United States—Social life and customs—Juvenile literature. I. Title. II. Title: Growing up on a farm in the long ago.
S521.5.A2R56 2011
630.973'09034—dc23 2011020881

Printed in the United States of America
11 12 13 14 15 16 17 18 19 / 9 8 7 6 5 4 3 2 1

Texas Tech University Press
Box 41037 | Lubbock, Texas 79409-1037 USA
800.832.4042 | ttup@ttu.edu | www.ttupress.org

Manufactured by Thomson-Shore, Dexter, MI (USA); RMA576KJ426, September, 2011

FOR RICKY

CONTENTS

CONTENTS

ILLUSTRATIONS

ACKNOWLEDGMENTS

Many thanks to all of you who made writing this book possible—from the friends who cheered me on, to my department chair, Charles Dobbs, who encouraged this undertaking, to Judith Keeling, who saw the possibilities of a book about children's history for children. A special thanks to my mother, Mary Riney, who introduced me to books. Thank you to Scott Riney and Roberta Trites for early readings and good suggestions. I also extend a very special thank you to Ruth Barton, who suggested way back in 1984 that I should write this book. I'm just sorry it took me this long to write it. Most of all, I thank the two men in my life who inspire everything I do, Rick and Ricky Kehrberg.

ALWAYS PLENTY TO DO

INTRODUCTION

Growing Up on a Farm The Way It Used to Be

When my mamma was sick of course I had to do the housework. I had to make supper. I also had to do the scrubbing, and thought it was fun to scrub. My papa killed a chicken and I dressed it and made mamma chicken soup. Mamma said it tasted good. She said I was doing pretty well.

RUTH LANDWEHR, AGE 11[1]

Every Saturday I help my father husk corn. One evening he allowed me to shovel out the load. My little brother and sister unloaded the wagon for me one time. They threw the ears out with their hands and no one told them to do it. They had been playing in the corn and kept throwing out the ears until the wagon was empty. My brother is six and my sister is four.

JAMES SMEJKAL, AGE 11[2]

Last summer I worked in the field and when I went to the field each day I could see how much the corn had grown. I plowed as much as my father did. One day when we were plowing a big storm came up and we were very much frightened and when I went to turn around I broke my plow. We fixed it and got back to where the buggy was and put it in and went home. When we got there mamma and grandma were after the chickens and I helped them.

MARIE TURPEN, AGE 12[3]

Ruth, James, and Marie were all born around 1900 and all grew up on farms. They each wrote a letter describing their lives to a newspaper called the *Nebraska Farmer*. Their stories tell about farm children growing up in the early years of the twentieth century. Each child had big responsibilities, and each was a hard worker. Ruth, James, and Marie lived in a world where children were very important to their families, who could not have managed without them.

These children grew up very differently from children today. Imagine growing up in a time when children worked nearly as much as grown-ups, where school was less important than work, and where children had to create own fun. Imagine having only two or three changes of clothes to wear and only one pair of shoes. Imagine making your own clothes, growing the vegetables and fruit for your meals, and being responsible for helping your parents—all tasks that started when you were very young. In this world there were no televisions, no computers, no indoor toilets, no running water, and no microwave ovens. Most people had never traveled farther than twenty miles in a single day, and most people went places by walking or by riding on a horse or in a wagon. This world was very different from the world you live in today.

Even though it might sound strange, this world existed right here in the United States. Between the end of the Civil War in 1865 and the end of World War I in 1918, most farm children worked hard, went to school when they could, and played with homemade toys. They and their parents lived with far less than what most people have today. Children helped their parents with making the clothes they wore and the food they ate and with doing all of the chores required on the farm. Even going to school in the morning could require a two-mile hike across fields, through the woods, and over a stream.

While life on a farm could be difficult, it was also rewarding. Everyone had jobs to do, including boys and girls, big and little. Just like Ruth, James, and Marie, children were proud of the work they did on their parents' farms. Most children began the day with chores before school in the morning. After breakfast, if their parents did not need them at home, they went to a one-room schoolhouse to study math, reading, and writing. During recess, often their favorite time of the day, children played on the playground with the other boys and girls. And when they went home at night, there were other chores to do, like feeding the animals again and milking the cows. The meal had to be cooked, and the dishes had to be washed by hand after dinner. During any time left over, farm children played with their toys or enjoyed games. Farm children's days were very busy, filled with work, school, and play.

This book is about how farm children's lives were different long ago. It is about what children wore, what they ate, the kinds of houses they lived in, the kinds of bathrooms they used, and the tools that they and their mothers used to make breakfast, lunch, and dinner. The book is about the work children did, what they studied in school, and what they liked to do when they had time to play. This story tells how important children were to their families and how much children's lives have changed in the last one hundred years.

1
LIVING ON A FARM
Making Food, Clothes, Homes, and Medicine from Scratch

Food and Farm Families

Rose Wilder Lane's Missouri Childhood[1]

Rose Wilder Lane, the daughter of Almanzo Wilder and Laura Ingalls Wilder (the famous writer), grew up on her parents' farm in the Missouri Ozarks. In 1894, when she was eight years old, her family left the state of South Dakota and headed to Missouri. Times had been hard in South Dakota because of drought, grasshoppers, and illness, and Rose's parents thought they should start over again on a farm in Missouri. They wanted to live someplace where they could grow most of the food they needed.

Rose and her parents traveled south to Missouri in a covered wagon. There was very little room for their belongings in the wagon, so they left behind anything that was not absolutely necessary. Traveling this way was crowded and difficult, and their wagon moved very slowly. The Wilders camped out along the way because there were very few hotels, and they, like most families, could not afford to stay in one even if they found one nearby. Instead, the Wilders and other families like them brought along their own supplies, sleeping and cooking out in the open.

Rose's family brought some food with them from South Dakota, and some food they found along the way. As the family prepared for their trip, Rose's mother, Laura, made hardtack to eat as they traveled. Hardtack was "white and flat and round, as large and as hard as a plate," made from flour, water, and salt. It was a very large, very hard, very salty cracker. It lasted a long time and did not need to be stored in a refrigerator. Rose wrote, "You could not possibly bite or chew" hardtack. Instead, the family broke off pieces with a hammer and soaked the pieces in tea to make them soft enough to eat. From their farm in South Dakota, they also brought kernels of wheat in big buckets. When she was hungry, Rose chewed on grains of wheat, commenting that "it was good to eat, but hard to chew. It takes so long to chew a mouthful into paste that you can swallow, that you can eat wheat all day and still be hungry." She and her family also gathered wild foods from alongside the road, including plants such as sheep sorrel, dandelion leaves, and hazelnuts, and ate sheep sorrel and dandelion leaves like lettuce in salads. Sometimes Rose's father shot a rabbit or a crow and the family ate rabbit or crow stew for dinner. When her father could, he worked for farmers along their way south and traded his work for food such as potatoes, corn, cucumbers, eggs, and milk.[2]

When the Wilders arrived in Missouri, they were poor and had to be very careful not to waste food. Because they were poor, the food that Rose took to school was very plain. She remembered later, "I carried a small tin lunch pail with an apple in it and several slices of brown bread spread with bacon fat, as we were too poor to have butter." Rose was so embarrassed about eating bacon fat on her bread that she sat alone so no one could see what she was eating. Sometimes, Rose's mother put a surprise in her lunch, a raw carrot or a small pie made with a filling of milk and a little bit of sugar. Even an apple could be special. "Sometimes the apple was cut in two without cutting the skin in any way—which is very surprising when you peel the apple and find it in halves already, but simple to do when you know how."[3] (See the end of the chapter to find out how to slice an apple without peeling it!) At the end of the day, after dinner, the family sat in front of the stove and ate popcorn while they read books together.

Although Rose and her family had to work long and hard, their farm in Missouri was soon producing lots of good things to eat: chickens and eggs, milk and butter, corn, wheat, and oats, strawberries, grapes, and many, many apples. They never again had to worry about having enough food, and Rose never again ate bacon fat on her bread.

If you stepped back in time and visited a farm in 1900, you would see a very different world from the one you live in. The food didn't come from a box or a can but from the garden or the henhouse. Most of the clothes people wore were homemade too, and the houses were small and cramped. All around you, boys, girls, mothers, and fathers worked, doing the day's chores and making their home a good place to live.

Just like it was for Rose Wilder Lane, food was a very important part of every farm child's day.

Mothers prepared food in kitchens that were very different from the kitchens we have today. Most kitchens had no running water and definitely no dishwashers. There were no refrigerators and freezers and no microwaves. In that kitchen was a stove that burned coal or wood for heat, a basin that could be filled by hand with water for washing, and a table that was used like today's countertop. Mothers fixed most of the food that their families ate, and children, especially girls, helped. Children ate breakfast, lunch, and dinner, just like children today, but what they ate was often very different. Cooking took a lot more time than it does today because mothers and children cooked meals from scratch, beginning with basic ingredients such as flour, sugar, milk, and eggs to make the meal. When they baked a cake, they did not have a mix from a box that already had those ingredients. So usually someone in each family had to work almost all day to make three meals.

When children got out of bed in the morning, they smelled breakfast cooking and knew that their mothers were already working. Because all of the family worked hard on a farm, everyone needed to begin the day with a big breakfast. In the morning, children often ate hot cereal such as oatmeal, cornmeal mush, or grits. Mothers mixed oats, cornmeal, or corn grits with boiling water and salt and cooked them until thick. Sometimes children ate their hot cereal plain, and sometimes they ate it with milk, butter, bacon grease, or sugar. On other days, mothers mixed up pancakes, fried them on the stove, and served them with some kind of syrup, like maple syrup, sorghum, or molasses. Other times, mothers baked biscuits and covered them with gravy made from sausage, sausage grease, flour, and milk. A good, hot breakfast was the best way to start a busy day.

For most families, lunch (they might call it dinner) was the biggest meal of the day. Everyone who was at home came to the table to eat, including mothers, fathers, and children who weren't at school. The whole family had been working hard all morning and planned to work hard all afternoon, so lunch needed to be a big, nutritious meal. For lunch, Mothers usually fried some sort of meat, often salt pork. (Salt pork is a lot like bacon without as much pink meat.) Mothers sliced the salt pork, cooked it in a pan with a little water, then took it out, coated it in flour or cornmeal, and fried it again to make it crispy. Then they could make gravy out of the grease left in the pan. Fried salt pork and cornbread or biscuits might make up the whole lunch meal. Potatoes were also an important food, particularly in the winter. Mothers baked, boiled, mashed, or fried potatoes or other vegetables such as parsnips and turnips. In late spring, summer, or fall when the garden was growing, there might also be green beans or peas or tomatoes or other fresh vegetables to eat too. On special days like Sundays and holidays, a family often ate fried chicken, pork chops, or roast beef.

When children came home from school and before they started their chores, they might eat a snack, which was also homemade. Children often ate bread and butter and jam or a piece of cornbread with butter. Mothers didn't always have time to bake cookies, but if they did, children might have those as an after-school snack. If the family grew fruit trees, there were apples. The snacks weren't very big, though, because dinner would be ready soon.

Dinner (some families called it supper) was the last meal of the day and often smaller than lunch. Bean soup or baked beans were good warm meals, and mothers usually served these with homemade bread. Sometimes, if everyone was very tired from working, there might just be bread and milk for dinner. Baked apples with cinnamon and sugar were a special treat when it was cold outside, but desserts were only for special occasions because sugar was very expensive.

Ice cream was the most special dessert of all and almost always eaten in the summertime. Farm families did not have refrigerators, which made making ice cream more difficult, because someone usually had to go to town to buy ice. While waiting for the ice, the mother made a mixture of eggs, milk, cream, and flavorings, all the ingredients of ice cream. Once the block of ice had arrived, it was chipped and broken into pieces, mixed with salt, and put into an ice cream freezer. The ice cream mixture was poured into a canister and the canister lowered into the salt and ice. Then the freezer had to be cranked and cranked until the ice cream froze in the canister. When the ice cream was firm and cold, it was then scooped out into bowls and eaten. Every last bit had to be eaten all at once because there was no refrigerator and no way to keep the ice cream frozen until the next day. So everyone ate and ate until all the ice cream was gone.

Making meals required lots of effort on `everyone's part. Because families didn't have much money, they did their best to be self-sufficient, which means that they tried to grow as much of the food they ate as possible. If families wanted to eat green beans and tomatoes and watermelons in the summer, they had to grow them in a garden. If they wanted to eat vegetables in the winter, they planted potatoes, carrots, onions, turnips, and other vegetables able to last for a long time without

The White family milking, ca. 1903. This family lived on a farm near Manhattan, Kansas, and delivered and sold their milk in town. *FK2.R5.751*1. Courtesy of the Kansas State Historical Society, Topeka, Kansas.*

refrigeration. These vegetables, called root vegetables, sat in a cool cellar all winter. Some kinds of squash, like pumpkins and acorn squash, lasted all winter too. If a family wanted to have apples in the winter, they needed to grow them during the summer, and they stored the apples in the cellar with the potatoes and other vegetables. If a family grew berries and other fruit, they could make them into jams, jellies, and preserves to eat on bread and biscuits all winter long. In the summer, children often went to the woods and open fields to pick wild fruit such as plums, blackberries, and currants. They even made watermelon rinds and green tomatoes into jams and jellies. It was important not to waste anything!

Farm families also raised animals for meat. They raised hogs to slaughter in the fall, cut them into hams and chops, and made other parts into sausages and bacon. Cattle and sheep could be slaughtered for meat too, and families usually waited for cold weather to slaughter animals so that the meat would not spoil. Some kinds of meat, like ham and bacon, were smoked so that they would last through the year. Sausage and pork chops could be cooked, packed into crocks, and the hot fat from cooking the meat poured over them so when the fat cooled and hardened, it formed a barrier to keep the air out and the meat fresh and safe to eat. Just like with fruit and vegetables, families tried not to waste anything. Some families ate pickled pigs' feet and snouts, and hogs' intestines made good casings for sausages or could be cleaned, fried, and eaten. Other families saved all of the blood from butchering and used it to make sausages and puddings that were full of protein.

Hunting and fishing were also important ways to get meat. Families often ate deer, rabbits, and birds like ducks and geese. One Texas boy remembered how much he liked to eat catfish. "When the fish were washed and cut up, my mother took the pieces and rolled them in cornmeal. Then she put them in a skillet of hot lard. First there was the sound of frying, and then the smell of fish frying. . . . I got the first piece off the skillet . . . With corn bread and buttermilk it was enough for supper."[4]

Most families also raised chickens that laid eggs. When the chickens were too old to lay eggs, they were eaten as fried chicken or in chicken and dumpling dinners. Usually families also had cows that gave milk, which children drank and their mothers and older sisters made into cheese and butter. The crops that fathers raised, such as corn and oats, could be fed to animals or turned into bread and cereal for the family's meals. The family might also grow wheat, which could be ground and baked into bread.[5]

Although most food was homemade, some food items couldn't be made at home and had to be bought at the store. These included sugar, spices, flavorings, and other ingredients used for baking, like baking powder and yeast. Sometimes mothers traded eggs or butter for groceries at the store.

Like food, clothing was often homemade. Mothers made most of the clothing that children wore, and girls often helped. To make clothes, mothers and girls bought fabric at the store, used a pattern to mark the fabric, cut out the pieces, and sewed

Marion Ritchie with chickens, ca. 1912. This farm girl lived in Shawnee County, Kansas. *FK2.S5.751*5. Courtesy of the Kansas State Historical Society, Topeka, Kansas.*

the pieces into shirts, dresses, and other types of clothing, all tasks they almost always had to do by hand. Sometimes mothers used sewing machines, but because of no electricity, even sewing with a machine took work. The person sewing used a foot to push on a lever (called a treadle) to make the needle go up and down through the fabric.

One hundred years ago, children had only a few clothes, usually no more clothes than they absolutely needed. They had an outfit for school, some good clothes to wear to church, and old clothes for work. A boy might have two or three pairs of pants and two or three shirts, and a girl might have two or three dresses. People didn't have closets in their houses because they didn't have enough clothes to fill them. Instead, a few nails behind the door held all of their clothes. Once a dress a shirt or a pair of pants was no longer good enough for church or school, it became work clothing. Children also often handed down clothing, with the younger children wearing clothes that had become too small for the older children to wear. Clothes that were completely worn out became cleaning rags, patches, or rag rugs. Families wasted nothing.

Girls almost always wore dresses because it was not considered modest for girls to wear pants. Most of the older girls wore dresses that hung down below their knees, long enough to touch the tops of their shoes, but little girls usually wore dresses that came up almost to their knees. Most dresses were dark colored—gray, black, brown, or dark blue—because those colors were less likely to show dirt, and dark-colored fabric cost less than bright colors such as red, purple, and pink. To keep their clothing clean and protected while they worked and played, the girls wore aprons over their dresses.

Sometimes, girls wore dresses that were made out of feed sacks! The food for chickens and other animals came in large cloth sacks, and those sacks

Wisconsin girls in matching dresses, all made from the same material, ca. 1900. Mothers could save money by buying large quantities of a single material to make their daughters' dresses. *Courtesy of the Wisconsin Historical Society, Madison, Wisconsin.*

were often printed with special patterns and bright colors. When buying feed, Mothers tried to make sure that they had enough sacks in a certain color or pattern so they could make inexpensive dresses for their daughters. Girls always wore petticoats under their dresses, and sometimes those were made out of sacks too. Flour, sugar, and some seeds came in plain white cotton sacks with advertisements printed on them. Mothers used bleach to remove the printing and then sewed the sacks into petticoats and other types of underclothing. Those same sacks made good cloth diapers for babies. (Disposable diapers hadn't been invented yet.)

During the winter, both girls and boys wore long, woolly underwear under their clothing. Although scratchy and uncomfortable, this warm underwear was absolutely necessary. The coats children wore were not very warm, so it was very important to wear lots of layers of clothing. Girls also usually wore heavy wool stockings and high-buttoned shoes that came up over their ankles.

When the weather was warm, though, boys and girls went barefoot. Shoes were even more expensive than clothing, and children tried to keep their shoes nice for as long as possible by wearing them only when needed or when going to church. Even in summer, girls wore long skirts, long sleeves, and sunbonnets when they went outside. Getting a tan, freckles, or a sunburn was not fashionable because it made a girl look like she had to work hard out of doors. For girls, working outside in the hot sun was not fashionable.

Boys were more likely than girls to have store-bought clothing. Many boys wore overalls for school and work, and overalls were less expensive to buy than to make. Overalls were usually blue or blue-and-white striped. At other times, boys wore dark-colored pants and a shirt, with suspenders to hold up their pants. Mothers made most of their shirts, using the same sort of material that they used for girls' dresses. Sometimes a mother, with lots and lots of clothes to make, bought yards and yards of one kind of fabric and made everyone's clothing out of the same material. As a result, everyone in the family—boys and girls, big and little—had clothes that matched. Unlike boys today, farm boys always worked wearing long pants and long-sleeved shirts and hats with broad brims. These kept the sun off their arms, legs, and faces and kept them from getting sunburned. Sunscreen hadn't been invented yet.

Children did not usually have special clothes for special purposes. For example, most people did not own swimming suits. When girls went swimming, they wore their oldest dresses without the petticoats underneath. When boys and girls went

A family from Buffalo County, Nebraska, and their log cabin, ca. 1904. Photograph by Solomon Butcher. *RG2608. PH: 0706. Courtesy of the Nebraska State Historical Society, Lincoln, Nebraska.*

swimming together, boys wore their old pants. But when boys went swimming with other boys and there were no girls around, they wore nothing! When the children went out to play, they wore their work clothes, so it didn't matter as much if they got dirty or torn. Even so, their mothers wanted them to be careful, since mending had to be done by hand.

It wasn't just food and clothing that was homemade. Houses were homemade too. Families built their own houses to save money. In places where there were forests, families could build their houses out of logs. Families built log houses by cutting down trees, removing the branches, and smoothing the long, straight logs. The builders cut notches in the logs so that they could be stacked one on top of the other, with as small a gap between the logs as possible. Then the gaps between the logs were filled with clay, mud, or some other sort of soft material that could be packed into the cracks. The builders then put a roof on top of the stacked logs, making a snug, warm house.

Other families settled in areas such as western Kansas, Nebraska, or Texas where there weren't any forests. Even so, families found a way to build their houses without logs and lumber. One kind of house that they built was called a dugout. A dugout was exactly what it sounds like: a house dug out of

Children from Norton County, Kansas, in front of a dugout between 1880–1890. This home was made of many materials available in the environment, like dirt, logs, sod, and rock. *FK2.N4.75*6. Courtesy of the Kansas State Historical Society, Topeka, Kansas.*

the earth. To build a dugout, the family cut a hole about eight feet long and about eight to twelve feet wide, deep into a hill or a bank. Once the hole was dug, the family used logs, wood, or sod to build a front wall and then reinforced the roof with branches. The dugout was really just a large cave, and a family with five or six children might have as much room in their whole house as you have in your bedroom! A house like this was very small, dark, and cramped, but it was warm in the winter, cool in the summer, and very inexpensive to build. All it cost was the time that it took to build it.

Another inexpensive house that people built in areas without many trees was a sod house. In order to build a sod house, the family cut strips of prairie grass and earth, leaving the roots attached. These strips were about two feet wide and ten to twelve feet long. In order to build a wall, strips were piled one on top of another until they were tall enough to make a wall. This process was repeated four times to build four walls. Doors and windows were cut into the sod, and the roof was made of whatever type of material was available. Sometimes the builders laid poles on top for a roof and more sod put on top of that. As a result, grass and flowers might even grow above people's heads! These houses could be as small as a dugout or as big as a modern house, but most were no more than twelve feet long and twenty feet wide, about the size of a living room or family room today. Some families put glass windows into dugouts and sod houses, but these were very expensive, and not everyone could afford them. Sometimes the holes for the windows were just left wide open, with nothing in them. If a family wanted to keep out the bugs and the wind but still have some light, they hung cloth or greased paper in the windows. Just like dugouts,

Family from Custer County, Nebraska, in front of a sod house, ca.1900. This sod house was unusually large and had more than one room. The family also owned a windmill, which helped them pump water from the ground. *Photograph by Solomon Butcher. RG2608.PH:1380. Courtesy of the Nebraska State Historical Society, Lincoln, Nebraska.*

sod houses were warm in the summer, cool in the winter, and very, very inexpensive. All materials were right there on the farm.

In some places, there was very little wood, and families didn't have enough time to build a dugout or a sod house. In that case, they might build a claim shanty. A claim shanty was a tiny, one-room house made out of a single layer of boards. Sometimes people lined the walls of claim shanties with heavy red or blue paper to keep the wind out. These houses were very cold in the winter and hot in the summer because there was only one thin layer of boards between the family and the weather outside. In the winter, children sometimes woke up in the morning and found snow and ice on their beds.

If a family made a profit in farming, they might someday have a nice, large house built of wood, brick, or stone, a house with real glass windows. This was a goal that most families worked for, and it might take them five or ten years to achieve their goal. Even so, these houses were much smaller than what people live in today. Often, houses did not have dining rooms, living rooms, or family rooms. A house might just have three or four rooms: a large kitchen, a sitting room, and one or two bedrooms. Most children did not have their own rooms but shared their rooms, and even their beds, with their brothers or sisters. Babies and small children usually slept with their parents. Most houses did not have furnaces for heat, so it was important to sleep close to brothers and sisters to stay warm.

Very few houses had running water that came out of a faucet. Instead, someone had to carry water from a pump or a well in order to do the cooking and the cleaning. Pumps and wells were usually closer to the barn than the house since the horses and cows needed water several times a day. Pumping water was hard work. Boys and girls pushed a lever up and down, over and over, to get enough water for the family to use. Water was also very heavy to carry, so bringing water to the house was a difficult and important chore.

Most houses did not even have bathrooms! Children washed their faces by pouring warm water into a big bowl and then scrubbing with a piece of cloth and homemade soap. Several children might even share the same water. Most children took their baths in the kitchen just once a week. The mother or father placed a big tub in the kitchen in front of the stove and heated water in kettles on top of the stove. The hot water was then poured into the tub so the children could take their baths. Because carrying water was such hard work and heating water on a wood or coal stove took so much time, children often shared the bathwater. Mothers bathed babies first, and then older brothers and sisters all bathed. At the end of the evening, the parents threw the dirty, soapy water outside to water plants. The bathwater might even be used to clean the floor. Wasting water meant wasting precious time and energy, so even dirty water had to be used again.

Farmhouses did not have indoor toilets either, so everyone had to go to the backyard and use an outhouse or privy. The privy was a little house with a pit dug underneath it. A bench with a few holes cut in it was over the pit, and that was where everyone sat. This was their toilet. At night, if it was very cold or rainy or snowy, people might use a chamber pot (a big, wide mug with a handle) which was stored under the bed at night and dumped into the pit in the privy in the morning. Most families did not buy toilet paper either. It was too expensive to buy something that would be thrown away after just one use. Instead, they used dried corncobs with the kernels removed or paper pages from old store catalogs. Many years ago, catalogs were not made out of slick, shiny paper. Instead, they were made of the same kind of paper used in phone books or newspapers today. One man who grew up on a ranch remembered using "small bundles of grass, corn cobs, corn husks, rags, and water," instead of toilet paper.[6] Those corncobs and corn husks must have been uncomfortable to use!

Children did not usually have toothbrushes or use toothpaste. Instead, they used a finger, a stick, or a rag dipped in baking soda or salt and rubbed across their teeth. (Ask your parents and try this sometime. It won't taste very good, but your teeth will be clean and shiny). Children had to be careful to keep their teeth clean and healthy. Most children only saw dentists for toothaches, and then the dentist pulled out the teeth if they had cavities.

While farm children lived in homemade houses, ate homemade food, and wore homemade clothing, their parents also treated their illnesses with homemade medicine. Seeing a doctor was very expensive, and families only called a doctor when someone was hurt badly or was very sick. Doctors often came to the house instead of patients going to their office or the hospital. Doctors sometimes even did complicated things, like taking out tonsils, on the kitchen table! To prepare the room, the mother scrubbed down the walls and the table and boiled the scalpel and other instruments in a pan of water on the stove.

Colds and sore throats received simple treatment at home. Gargling with saltwater was a common way to make sore throats feel better. If a boy or a girl with a cold had a stuffy nose and was having a hard time breathing, the mother might mash up a raw onion or fry it, wrap it in a piece of cloth, and put it on the child's chest. The fumes from the onion helped the child breathe more easily. If that didn't work to help the child breathe, turpentine (a very smelly liquid) could be mixed with goose fat and spread on a child's chest. Mothers also treated colds and stuffy noses by mixing ground dried mustard with water and spreading it on a boy's or girl's chest. For upset stomachs, mothers used a remedy of tea and toast. They tried to help children avoid getting colds, sore throats, earaches, and upset stomachs by hanging cloves of garlic or bags of a very smelly herb called asafetida around their necks. This method probably worked because it scared other children away with its bad smell. Sick children kept their germs to themselves.

Mothers used other remedies for different problems. Soaking in hot water was the way to mend a sore foot or a sprained ankle although mothers sometimes put a piece of salt pork on a wound and wrapped it in cloth. People thought that the raw meat caused swelling to go down or an infection to disappear. Sometimes it worked, and sometimes it didn't. Raw potato, baking soda, or the gel from an aloe vera plant soothed burns. Bee stings were treated by covering the stung area with mud, and a spider web placed across a cut could help to stop bleeding. Mothers also stitched deep cuts together with needle and thread if a doctor was not there to do it.

Children suffered with some illnesses that they

don't usually get today. Now, children get shots that help prevent diseases like measles, mumps, diphtheria, whooping cough, and chicken pox. Some of these diseases, like diphtheria and whooping cough, could kill children who became ill with them. Other diseases, like chicken pox, were uncomfortable but usually not really dangerous. Doctors didn't have as many medicines or as many tools available to them as they have today. In fact, when a doctor came to the house, all of his tools and medicine fit into one little bag, smaller than a school backpack. There were no X-rays, CAT scans, or MRIs.

Sometimes the only way to keep everyone healthy was to keep sick people away from people who were healthy. If someone in a family did get a serious disease such as the measles, the family placed themselves in quarantine. They put a sign by the road, telling everyone that somebody was ill. Friends and neighbors who had not had the disease stayed away until all were well. If a family was quarantined, the children could not go to school until all of their brothers and sisters were healthy again. If many of the children in a school were sick, the whole school closed until everyone was healthy, which was a way to keep other children from becoming sick. One Kansas farm boy wrote in his diary: "There were several of the children that had been going to school are sick. Mother was afraid that it was something contagious. So none of us went to school."[7] Even though illnesses occurred, most farm children lived healthy lives, and most of them lived to be adults. They ate good food, worked in the sunshine, and got lots of exercise. Everyone tried to stay healthy so that the family could keep working.

Long ago, farm children's lives were much different from those of children today. Probably the most important difference was that nearly everything was done by hand, and almost every job, big or small, took lots of hard work. Parents and children worked together to make their meals, sew their clothing, and build their homes. Even staying healthy was an important thing that children learned to do for themselves. They learned to be responsible and willing to do lots of important chores around the house and the farm.

Here's how to slice an apple without peeling it. First, find a small, clean apple and a long, clean needle. Holding on tight to the blunt end of the needle, push it into the side of the apple in the middle. Sweep the needle from side to side, being sure not to poke any more holes in the apple's skin. The needle will cut through the flesh of the apple, leaving just a small hole where you pushed the needle in. When you peel the apple, you will find that it is already cut in half.

2
WORKING ON A FARM
Weeding, Milking, and Threshing

Learning to Work

Ralph Moody and Life on a Colorado Farm[1]

Ralph Moody was born in 1898 in New Hampshire, but when he was eight years old, his family moved to Colorado. His father was sick with a lung disease called tuberculosis, and the doctors thought that the clean air and dry climate in Colorado would help make him strong. The family bought a farm in what is now Littleton, Colorado, and set about making a home for themselves. Many years later, Ralph wrote about his life and recalled all of the different kinds of work he did on the farm to help his parents.

Ralph's family had never been to Colorado

before and had never even seen their house before they moved into it. It was a big surprise, and not a good one. Ralph later remembered, "The chimney was broken off at the roof and most of the windows were smashed. When we turned off the wagon road, a jack rabbit leaped out from under the house and raced away through the clumps of cactus and soapweed."[2] When she first saw the house, his mother wanted to cry, but she didn't. Making the house fit to live in and the farm support a family was going to require work from everyone.

As soon as he could, Ralph began working to earn money and help his parents. In the beginning, he earned twenty-five cents a day herding a neighbor's cattle. Riding a horse and being a cowboy might sound like fun, but Ralph soon learned that the work was much more difficult than he thought. The cows did not want to be herded, and his horse, Ned, did not want to run after the cattle. "I beat the tar out of Ned, trying to make him go fast enough so that I could keep them rounded up, but the most I could get out of him was that clumping trot. While I was driving back a few stragglers on one side, others would head for Carl Henry's oat field on the run. When I came back with the first bunch that tried it, I found that I only had nineteen cows left in the herd—the rest had got away over one of the hills."[3] Ralph eventually learned how to herd the cattle and make them go where he wanted them to go. He gave the money he earned to his parents.

Ralph also helped his father with other chores such as cutting hay. One day when he was cutting hay, a train whistle scared the horses pulling the hay rake, and they began to run. The hay rake broke, and the horses dragged Ralph behind because he was too scared to let go of the lines. As he later remembered, "About all there was left of my blouse was the collar band, and both legs got ripped off my overalls."[4] He was covered with cuts and bruises, and he had broken nine of his toes. The doctor came to the farm, straightened Ralph's broken toes (without any anesthesia), and taped his feet to two shoe-shaped boards so that they could heal. Two weeks later, Ralph was back haying, with the bottoms of his feet protected by the boards. Not even nine broken toes could keep him from working and helping his family.

Even though they worked hard, Ralph's family was not successful at farming. There was never enough water for their crops, and they decided that it was a better idea to move into town where there were jobs for Ralph's father. When Ralph was only twelve, his father became ill with pneumonia following an accident between his horse and an automobile. The horse had never seen a car before and panicked, throwing Ralph's father out of his buggy and onto the ground. Even though he thought he was only slightly injured, he became ill and died. After his father's death, all of the lessons Ralph had learned on the farm about hard work became very important since his mother needed him to work and help support his five brothers and sisters. Just as it had been on the farm, everyone had to work in order to buy food, pay rent, and supply everybody with shoes and clothes. Ralph pulled dandelions for neighbors for ten cents an hour, herded cattle, and went door-to-door selling food that his mother had cooked. He had to be the man of the family, and he made his mother proud of the work he did and all of the support he gave her.

In most families today, the father and mother earn most or all of the money to support the family. Work is a parent's job, and going to school is a child's job. However, one hundred years ago, the work that farm children like Ralph Moody did was important to help support their families. Fathers did most of the heavy work on the farm, such as plowing or caring for large animals. They were also responsible for the business of the farm, such as buying and selling grain and going to the bank or the store. Mothers were usually responsible for the household chores—raising children, doing laundry, cooking food, and sewing clothing, among other jobs. Mothers also usually took care of chickens, milked cows, and made butter. When there was a lot of work such as planting or harvesting to be done in the fields, mothers worked in the fields beside fathers. But there was still plenty of work left to do. Fathers could not do all of the work in the fields by themselves, and mothers did not have enough time to do all of the work in the house either. As a result, children were important for helping their parents keep the family farm running.[5]

It was particularly important for children to be useful because farming was such a risky business financially. Nothing was guaranteed. Families planted their crops and gardens and raised their animals, but so much could go wrong. Growing crops needed enough rain and enough sunshine and enough time to grow, without late or early frosts. What crops didn't need were hailstorms, high winds, and very dry weather, all of which could destroy them, leaving a family with little or nothing to eat or to sell. When the weather was bad for crops, everyone worried. John Norton, growing up on his parents' farm in Kansas, wrote in his diary, "Rain! Rain! Will it never come? Everything is as dry as a bone. The crops are suffering badly."[6]

Bad weather wasn't the only problem for farmers. Insects such as locusts (locusts look a lot like grasshoppers, and people often called them grasshoppers) could swarm in and eat the crops. There were many summers in the late 1800s and early 1900s when farm families lost everything they were growing because of locusts. The insects arrived in enormous numbers forming huge clouds, and they dropped out of the sky like rain. They ate everything in sight. They ate the crops in the field and the vegetables in the garden, the clothes drying on the clothesline in the yard and the curtains in the windows. They even ate the wooden handles of rakes, hoes, and plows. They dropped into the wells, making the water taste terrible, but there was nothing else for the people to drink. When the locusts had eaten and spoiled everything they could, the swarms flew off to find more food, leaving hungry people and animals behind. The only happy animals were the chickens because they loved to eat locusts and considered them a great treat. Mammie Eberle, a Kansas farm girl, wrote in her diary about the damage that the locusts did. On

May 13, she wrote, "Grasshoppers taking everything," and on June 3, when she brought the laundry in from the line she noticed, "The Grasshoppers bit the clothes badly."[7] Farm families never knew when the crops would be good or when a disaster, like the locusts, would come and leave them hungry.

Because farm life was hard, each family member had to do his or her part. From the moment small children were old enough to follow directions, they began helping with chores around the house. Very small children usually helped their mothers because that work could be divided into small jobs that little children could do, like helping in the garden, planting, weeding, and picking vegetables. Little children also picked berries and fruit, and they helped in the henhouse, feeding chickens and gathering eggs. Another chore was the laundry. Sometimes the children pulled the basket of clean, wet clothes out to the laundry line in their wagons and helped their mothers by handing them wet clothes and clothespins so the mothers could put the newly washed clothes on the line to dry. In the kitchen, children helped wash and dry dishes, and while their mothers cooked, they brought the things needed for cooking. If the fire burned low, the children went out to the woodpile and brought in kindling, dried corncobs, or firewood. Because families had many children and because babies often got in a busy mother's way while she worked, older brothers and sisters, who were four, five, and six years old, often looked after babies and two- and three-year-olds while their mothers worked. In farm life, little children often had big responsibilities.

Once boys were old enough, they went into the fields to work side by side with their fathers. Depending on their families' needs, the boys might be eight, ten, or twelve years old. While little boys sometimes were able to put their work aside to play, older boys rarely got any time off from their tasks. An older boy's day began early with chores like feeding and carrying water to animals, bringing water into the house for his mother, and carrying wood in for the stove. Some boys milked cows, while others did not. (In some families boys milked, but in others, girls did the milking). Boys usually spent several hours every morning working before coming in for a big breakfast. After breakfast on a school day, the boy walked to the schoolhouse and spent the day studying. At the end of the day, he headed home to more chores.

Most boys stayed in school only until they were fourteen years old or had finished the eighth grade because parents needed them at home, helping on the farm. Farm boys did not expect to go to high school or college, and they could learn most of the math and reading that they needed to be farmers by the time they finished the eighth grade. Parents expected their sons to stay home and work on the farm until they were twenty-one years old. When a young man was twenty-one, his parents considered him to be an adult, and he had more choices about his life.

Boys who were at home, working for their parents, had plenty to do. Depending on the location of their farm and the types of crops the family grew, there was plenty of work year-round. In the Midwest in states like Iowa, Indiana, and Illinois, many farmers grew corn, and in the spring, a boy often stayed at home from school to help his father plant the crop. This work was long and tedious because the seeds had to be placed in the ground very carefully in long, straight rows. As the corn grew, the boys hoed between the rows to make sure that the weeds didn't grow up and choke the corn. In the fall, the corn was ready for harvesting. Until the 1940s, most families harvested corn by hand, pulling each ear off the stalk and throwing it into a wagon. Imagine walking slowly through a corn field, picking ear after ear, and tossing it over your shoulder into the wagon, row after long row. The weather was often cold when farm families picked corn, and boys (and girls too) might be out-

Wisconsin children harvesting corn, ca. 1904. Edgar and Jennie Krueger worked with their grandparents, aunts, and uncles to harvest the corn crop. Picking and carrying corn was something even small children could do. *Photograph by Alex Krueger, Krueger Family Collection. WHi-23934. Courtesy of the Wisconsin Historical Society, Madison, Wisconsin.*

side in freezing weather, helping with the harvest. This wasn't a job finished in a day. Sometimes picking the corn crop took weeks and weeks to finish.

When boys weren't tending the corn or other crops, they were helping their fathers take care of animals. Milking cows very early in the morning or late in the evening was hard work that made a child's hands very tired and sore. In the winter, the best part of that job was leaning against the warm side of a big cow, which was cozy on a cold morning. Many corn farmers also raised hogs because they ate and got fat on nearly any kind of food. Families saved all of the leftovers from dinner and any other scraps of food for the hogs, who ate almost anything, including potato peels, apple cores, watermelon rinds, and onion skins. All of the leftovers were boiled in a big pot and then taken out for the hogs to eat. Boys carried buckets full of slop, another word for leftovers, out to the hogs, morning and night, because slopping the hogs was regular boys' work. Boys also worked hauling cow and horse manure from the barns to spread on the fields as fertilizer. The manure smelled bad, and moving it out of the barn made arms and backs ache. Sometimes, though, if the weather was nice, a boy's parents might let him go and swim in a creek or a pond after hauling manure, just so he would be cleaner and less smelly when he came back into the house. Many, many jobs took a long time and were hard and had to be done under difficult conditions.

In other parts of the country, families depended on different crops, so boys had different kinds of work to do. If a family grew cotton, like farm fami-

Arkansas children, aged 10, 13, and 8, chopping cotton, ca. 1936. Note how two of them are working barefoot. *FSA-OWI Photographic Collection, LC-USF34-006345-D. Courtesy of the Library of Congress.*

lies did in many parts of Texas, Oklahoma, and Arkansas, even more work had to be done by hand. The farmers' routine started with planting, followed by weeding (or "chopping," as it was called), and then the picking season lasted from fall into winter. Pickers dragged long sacks of cotton behind them as they worked their way down the rows, picking cotton by hand, for there were no machines to pick cotton a hundred years ago. It was tiring work that made everyone's hands very sore.

If a family grew mostly wheat, as families in western Kansas and Nebraska, Colorado, and western Oklahoma and Texas often did, there was less work to be done by hand. Boys helped plant wheat in the fall or spring, depending on what kind of wheat their fathers were growing. Then they had to do some weeding, but the hardest work came in the summer and fall, during harvesting and threshing times. (Threshing means removing the grain from the stalk). Unlike picking corn and cotton, the work took place during a shorter period of time, and the families used more machines to do the job.

There was always work to do on the farm. If farmers had no work to be done in the fields, there was work to do with animals. If the crops and the animals didn't need care, then boys turned their attention to other chores like chopping wood, mending fences, and repairing machinery. If a family had cattle but could not afford to buy barbed wire for fences, boys herded cattle morning to night, sometimes staying out all night on their own, keeping the cattle on their land and safe from wolves, coyotes, and other animals that might harm them. Whatever their fathers needed them to do, the boys did.

Most of the time, farm boys worked without being paid, but sometimes parents let their sons earn a little extra money for themselves. Many boys went trapping in the winter, hunting animals for the fur that could be sold, and the money was kept for the things a boy might want, like candy or games or a new baseball or mitt. Other boys raised animals or crops for themselves. Oliver Myers, who grew up in Iowa, owned animals and raised fruit trees. He sold his animals and fruit at a profit and saved the money for college. He, like other boys, sometimes worked in the summer for other farmers when the work at home was finished. But his work for his family always came first.[8]

As a girl grew older, she was able to do more and more of her mother's work. Older girls' work was a bit different than boys' work because girls often had to be more flexible than boys. They did chores inside the house, but they sometimes did work outside too. Most older girls attended school until they were fourteen and then helped their parents from the time they were fourteen until they got married. More girls than boys were able to continue beyond the eighth grade and go to high school because many went on to become schoolteachers, helping out their families with their wages. Therefore, their parents were more likely to let them stay in school a bit longer than their brothers.

Just about any work that their mothers did, older girls did too. They helped with all of the meals for their families, which meant making food from scratch over a hot stove. Girls were particularly proud when they learned how to bake their first pie or cake. When there was a little bit of extra sugar and a little bit of extra time, their mothers might let the girls make taffy or fudge. Older girls also spent a lot of time taking care of their younger brothers and sisters because their mothers were often too busy. Cleaning was also an older girl's job, so she scrubbed the floors, washed the dishes, and helped with the laundry.

Laundry was the chore that most girls dreaded the most. Because there was so much work to do on wash day, many girls missed school on Mondays, staying home to help their mothers. Because it took all day to wash a family's clothes, wash day began very early, with someone in the family either pumping water or drawing it from the well. Washing and rinsing a week's dirty clothes took many gallons of water, and the pump or well was often a long way from the house. All of that water had to be carried into the house or into the front yard, depending on where the family did the laundry. (Sometime, try carrying a big gallon bucket of water across your yard. When you are finished, imagine doing it another ten or twenty times like a girl did on a typical wash day.)

Once the water had been carried, it had to be heated in big copper boilers, a task requiring lots of firewood and lots of time. Women and girls boiled, rubbed, and scrubbed the clothes, doing whatever necessary to get the dirt out. Sometimes they even pounded them on rocks. Only families with lots of money had washing machines one hundred years ago. Even those washing machines needed water carried to them since nobody on a farm could just turn a handle and have hot water come out of the tap. Once the dirt was rubbed and scrubbed out of the clothes, girls wrung the water out of them by twisting the garments—and that was hard work too! They then hung the clothing on the line to dry. In the winter, girls might hang laundry indoors or hang it outside to "freeze dry" in the cold. There were no automatic clothes dryers to make the work easier.

This entire laundry process took all day, and

even then it wasn't over. The fabric used to make clothing years ago was much stiffer and very scratchy compared to today. Ironing made the clothing soft and comfortable to wear. Tuesday was ironing day, and girls helped their mothers iron the clothing—everything from pants and shirts to dresses. Even underwear and sheets had to be ironed.

Girls also usually learned to sew, which was very hard work since most families did not have sewing machines, and everything had to be sewn with tiny, even stitches. Girls were often proud of the skirts, dresses, and quilts that they sewed, but sewing could be very tiring, since it made their eyes teary and their necks ache. Even though mothers expected their daughters to learn to sew, girls weren't always good at it. Mammie Eberle grew up in northeastern Kansas, and by the time she was a teenager, she did most of her family's sewing. Her father was sick in bed, and her mother was much too busy to do all of the housework, so Mammie did most of the housework for her family, including the sewing. But her sewing was terrible. She wrote in her diary about how much she hated sewing and how hard it was. On an October day she wrote, "I have cut out and made a pair of pants for Will [her brother] and they do not fit very well. I sew real sorry." The next day, she "finished the boys coats and very glad I am too."[9] Even though Mammie did not like to sew and did not sew well, someone needed to do the job. And even though the pants and coats probably did not fit too well or look nice, her brothers had to wear them anyway. They had nothing else to wear and no extra money to buy clothes at the store.

A girl worked both inside the house and outside. Mammie Eberle explained in her diary just how much work there was for older girls to do:

> I have done the washing today and did not get it done until four o'clock. It is very cloudy and I am afraid it will rain before morning and as the clothes are too wet to bring in I shall have to leave them out. The wind is moaning so sadly that it makes me feel like crying but I still like to hear it. I went out to the cowpen to milk old Puss [the cow] and she did me the honor to kick the milk all over me.[10]

After Mammie had done the laundry all day long, she still had to milk the cow. On another June day she wrote, "Well I think I have spent a busy day. I rinsed and hung clothes out to dry, scrubbed all the tins and kitchen and porch, ironed and churned, sowed lettuce seed and planted some beans besides all of the other housekeeping work which I have to do . . . My feet are aching so badly that I do not know what to do with them."[11] It's no wonder that she often wrote in her diary that she was "very tired."

Even though some jobs were typically done by men and boys and others were typically done by women and girls, sometimes boys did girls' work, and girls did boys' work. The rule on the farm was that if a job needed doing, then someone had to do it, whether it was that person's usual work or not. The stories of two young people explain why this might happen.

When Ralph Wood was a young boy growing up in western Wisconsin, he regularly did work that other people might consider girls' work. He gathered eggs, worked in the garden, helped his mother in the house, and as more children were born to the family, Ralph helped take care of his younger brothers and sisters. He did these chores because his mother needed help, and Ralph had no sisters. Four children had been born in his family before him—two older brothers and two older sisters. In the normal course of events, Ralph and his brothers would have helped his father while Ralph's sisters would have helped his mother. But just before Ralph was born, both of his sisters died of a terrible disease called diphtheria. Therefore,

Ralph's father had three boys to help him, and Ralph's mother had no one to help her. So Ralph as the youngest worked with his mother and helped her because she needed him more than his father did.[12]

Something similar happened in the Swafford family. Growing up in western Kansas, Elsie Swafford was the oldest of six children. She had twin sisters who were three years younger than she, twin brothers who were another three years younger than the sisters, and one last sister born several years later. When Elsie was ten years old, her twin sisters were seven and her twin brothers were four. There was lots of work to be done in the fields, but the boys were not old enough to help her father. So until the boys were old enough, Elsie worked with her father instead of helping her mother with the sewing. She was her father's "right hand man," working in the fields with him, doing what she thought of as boys' work, even helping her father cut hay. Children like Ralph Wood and Elsie Swafford had to be flexible, helping where and when their parents needed them.[13]

Martha Farnsworth, who grew up in Kansas, also knew work was everybody's responsibility—not necessarily a boy's or a girl's. She wrote in her diary about the work she did. "In the morning sister Belle & I hitched up old 'Barney & Prince' to the

Wisconsin boy and corn binder, ca. 1900. This boy was doing a man's job of running a corn binder. *WHi-45050. Courtesy of the Wisconsin Historical Society, Madison, Wisconsin.*

wagon and hauled two Barrels of water about 1/2 mile from a nice Spring. We have to be Pa's 'boys' for we have no brothers and our wells are getting low so [we] have to haul water, sometimes."[14]

Farm work sometimes demanded that everybody, even neighbors, cooperate in order to achieve a common goal—survival. One time of year this idea was particularly apparent: threshing time. After a family harvested their wheat crop, the wheat had to be threshed. Threshing, a process that came after harvesting, separated the grain from the wheat stalk so that it could be ground into flour and eaten. By the 1890s, farmers used a very large machine called a threshing machine in order to separate the grains of wheat from the stalk. Most farmers did not own their own threshing machines but rented one when needed. But even this big machine could not do the work all by itself. A whole team of men and boys worked together to keep the process going: hauling fuel and water for the steam engine, feeding the wheat into the machine, clearing away the unnecessary straw from the stalks, and gathering up the grain and taking it to be stored or sold. Neighbor boys and men from other farms often came to help, and when the work was finished on one farm, they moved on to the next farm to help their neighbors. They worked all day, every day, for days on end.

Women and girls did their parts during threshing time too, for the men and boys needed good meals to keep them strong. Months and months before threshing time, mothers started planning the meals to cook for the work crew. The women decided how many chickens and eggs and what kind of fruit and vegetables they needed and began raising and growing them months in advance. When threshing time came, mothers worked with their daughters to make five meals a day: an early breakfast, a small lunch in the field, a big dinner at the house, a small, mid-afternoon lunch, and a smaller nighttime supper. The amount of food the working men needed was huge! For breakfast the men might have eggs, pancakes, ham, pie, and coffee. For a mid-morning lunch, the women usually made coffee, sandwiches, donuts, and cookies, and the girls and little boys carried the food to the fields for the workers. Dinner, the big meal served at noon, often included chicken, ham, beef, two or three kinds of vegetables, hot bread or rolls, and two or three kinds of pie, such as apple, rhubarb, or lemon. In the afternoon, there were more sandwiches and cookies or cake. Finally, for supper everyone usually had leftovers from lunch and lots more pie.

Cooking so many meals kept the women and girls busy from three or four in the morning until almost midnight. After every meal, when the girls had finished helping with the cooking, they washed mountains of dirty dishes by hand. The food was cooked on a wood stove, and the water for washing had to be heated on the same stove, which made the kitchen very hot and uncomfortable, sometimes over 120 degrees. Imagine the hottest summer day you've ever experienced, and then imagine it just a little hotter still. At threshing time, women and girls worked in the hot, hot house while the men and boys worked in the fields. Through cooperation and hard work, families had enough grain for the next year's bread and some to sell for a profit.

Children worked hard, and because families depended upon them so much, the boys and girls often did not get to go to school as much as today's children. In 1900, the laws about schooling were very different from those today. Now, children go to school from the time they are five or six years old until they are sixteen years old or graduate from high school. Today it is against the law for parents to keep their children at home to work instead of going to school, for we believe that what children need most in order to succeed in the world is a good education. In 1900 and before, not every state had laws that required children to go to school. Those states that did have laws usually only required children between the ages of seven and fourteen to attend school, or until they had graduated from the eighth grade. Even in states with laws requiring children's attendance, children could stay at home if their parents needed them to work on the farm.

The amount of work children did also affected the amount of time they had to play because work and school both came before play. If children wanted to have more time to play, then they needed to turn their work into play. Working with their brothers and sisters, children often turned chores into contests. They worked to see who could dig the most potatoes, husk the most corn, or gather the most strawberries. Eating strawberries while gathering them could be fun too.

Herding cattle also offered opportunities for fun since this task was often done on horseback. Hours spent herding cattle offered opportunities to watch the clouds, to see new and different plants and animals, and to go exploring. The Norton family lived in central Kansas, and several of the boys in the family helped out by herding cattle. While fourteen-year-old John Norton worked, he also hunted rabbits and antelope, looked for snakes, and found prairie chicken nests. There was always something new and exciting to see as he and his brothers crossed the open prairie. But even herding could become boring and cold eventually. John Norton wrote in his diary, "The cattle went away on the 5th of December . . . I leaped with joy."[15]

Some other kinds of work could become play just because it was so interesting. Boys in particular often liked threshing time because threshing machines were big, noisy, and full of all sorts of moving parts. These machines were often the largest and most complicated machines that the boys had ever seen, aside from locomotives on the railroad.

But no matter how hard children tried, some

work could not be turned into play, and just because their work was necessary did not always mean that the children liked to do the work—often they did not. Work made farm children tired, but it could also make them sad and angry if what they really wanted to do was go to school or go out to play. In their world everyone they knew worked—men, women, and children. However, children knew that without their help, their families would not be able to eat, have clothes to wear, or have a home in which to live. Children could be proud of the fact that they helped when their families needed them.

3
GOING TO SCHOOL
Reading, Reciting, and Spelling Bees

The Importance of Education

William A. Owens of Texas[1]

William Owens was born in 1905 on a farm near Pin Hook, Texas. His father died not long after he was born, leaving his mother to struggle to raise her children. Then William's grandmother came to live with them and help his mother run the household.

Going to school was always a problem for William because there was so much work to be done on the farm. William's school year began late and ended early because his mother needed him to do farm work. He remembered that in the spring and summer, "There was more work than all of us could do, and we went from daylight till dark six days a week."[2] On top of that, the little one-room school at Pin Hook had a very short school year, usually lasting only about three months because parents needed their children at home to work. Many of the students were like William's older brother, Cleaver. William recalled, "Cleaver had dropped out of school without complaining. He had been kept home so often that he could never keep up with the class anyway."[3]

William was also embarrassed to be so poor. He had to bring his own lunch to school and often had nothing more than cornbread to eat. He was so ashamed that he did not sit with the other students at lunch but hid in back of the schoolhouse. Sometimes he even had to go to school without shoes. One day he noticed that his teacher wore nice new shoes, and William realized what he wanted to do with the rest of his life. "I knew what I was going to do: I was going to be a teacher and wear good brown shoes every day in the week."[4] William realized teachers earned a regular paycheck and definitely earned more than William's poor farming family.

Getting enough education to be a teacher was a challenge for William Owens. His family wanted him to stay at home and work in the fields, but William wanted to leave home and earn money so he could afford to go to high school and college. While he worked in the fields or worked at one of his other jobs, he thought about school and about reading poetry. He memorized his favorite poems and "in the field, went over them again and again, studying how they might be a part of me. They would not, I knew, if I worked in the field and never went to school. All I could see ahead of me was day after day working in the field."[5] But what William wanted most of all was to go to school, so he worked and saved and studied on his own.

When he was sixteen, William passed an entrance test and was admitted to East Texas Teacher's College at Commerce, where he finished his high school degree and earned a teacher's certificate. From there, he went to Paris Junior College and Southern Methodist University. Eventually, he earned a Ph.D. at the University of Iowa and later taught English at Columbia University in New York City. William went on to write many books, such as *This Stubborn Soil* and *A Season of Weathering*, about his early years on the farm in East Texas. Getting an education took a lot of work, but for William Owens, education gave him the opportunity to leave picking cotton and begin doing things he really wanted to do, like teach and write books.

For children like William, school was a very important part of life. They went to school to learn reading, writing, and math, but they also went to school to see their friends and play during recess. Because farm children spent most of their time working, going to school was a welcome break from their busy everyday lives.

As mentioned earlier, in most places, the school year was shorter than it is today. Some children, like William and his brother, only went to school three or four months out of the year, while others went to school for nine months, like children today. In farming areas, students often had three terms of school during the year. The first term started in October so that children had time to help their parents with the harvest in late August and September, and the term ended in December. The second term lasted from December through April, and then small children sometimes had another school term in May and June while their older brothers and sisters worked.

When children got up in the morning, they knew they were going to walk to school, sometimes two or three or more miles. One girl who grew up on a Texas farm walked three miles to school every day, and she recalled those days. "Going to school we'd pick huckleberries in the fall and pick up hickory nuts and things. We had lots of fun walking to school. We just sort of meandered along

Kansas boys and donkey cart, ca. 1900.
By permission of Mary Riney.

down the trail."[6] Some lucky children who had a long way to go might have their own pony and buggy that they drove to school. They tied up the pony outside of the schoolhouse all day, going outside at recess and lunch to feed carrots or apples to their ponies. If the weather was wet or cold or snowy, sometimes fathers and older brothers and sisters brought children to school in a wagon or a sleigh, but that was unusual. Children did not ride buses to school until the 1920s, 1930s, or later.

Standing in the schoolyard, looking at the

school, children saw something very different from what children see today at their schools. Farm children attended one- and two-room schools, which sometimes had as few as two or three students or as many as fifty. A one-room schoolhouse was just what it sounds like—a building with one big room where all of the children studied together. Most of these schools were small, rectangular buildings with windows to let in the sunlight because there were no lamps or electric lights in the schools. Children entered by a door at one end of the building, or sometimes there were two separate doorways, one for girls and one for boys. Then they put their coats and hats on hooks in a small hallway just inside the door and left their lunches there all morning on a shelf.

When children came into the classroom, there were usually eight rows of desks from front to back, with an aisle down the middle of the room. Boys and girls sat on different sides of the room, and the smallest children sat at the front, the oldest at the back. In this way, children sat with their class, from the first grade through the eighth grade. In most places, there was no kindergarten, and students began school when they were six or seven and in the first grade.

The teacher sat at the front of the room at her own desk, facing the classroom. Behind the teacher's desk was a big blackboard where the students wrote their lessons. Somewhere in the classroom there was usually a big, cast-iron stove that provided heat in the winter. Some students, usually the little ones, sat very close to the stove, while the older children had to sit a long way from it. The classroom could get quite cold in the winter, so the teacher might let the students wear their coats or come up next to the stove to get warm as they needed. Since there was no water fountain in the classroom, when students needed a drink they drank water out of a bucket, using a dipper. Everyone drank out of the same bucket and used the same dipper, so if one person was sick, soon everyone was sick. When several students became sick, the teacher usually dismissed school until everyone was well again. Also, there was no indoor toilet. Instead, students used the privy out in back of the school, which usually had one side for boys and one side for girls.

Students brought many of the items that they needed for their lessons from home each day. Each student needed a slate, which was like a small blackboard that could be placed on the desk. In the 1800s, students wrote their lessons on these slates instead of using pencils and paper. Slates could be used again and again, but paper could only be used once. Only after 1900 did most students begin to use pencils and paper. For reading, writing, and arithmetic, students brought their books from home

One-room schoolroom in West Travis County, Texas, ca. 1900. The stove in the middle of the room kept students warm in winter, and students used the blackboard in the front of the room for lessons. *PICA 05875. Courtesy of the Texas History Center, Austin Public Library, Austin, Texas.*

and often used the same books their parents had used years before. Sometimes the school had a small collection of books—a little library—but not always, and sometimes a globe or a map or two. If the students wanted to listen to music, they all had to sing together. If they were lucky, their teacher played the piano. Schoolrooms back then were very different from schoolrooms today, with their computers, projectors, electric lights, televisions, and other equipment.

Students often went to school from nine in the morning until four in the afternoon, having walked to school after completing their morning chores and eating breakfast. A typical day at school began with some sort of opening. Once the students had entered the classroom and taken their seats, the teacher led them in singing a song or in saying the Pledge of Allegiance. Teachers also sometimes read a poem or a verse from the Bible to the students before they began their lessons. Classes began after that, with students studying reading and math before the first recess of the day. Spelling lessons usually came after recess.

A one-hour lunch followed spelling. Students almost always brought their food in a lunch-bucket from home. When students opened their lunch, they might discover biscuits with salt pork. Students could eat bread and meat or bread and butter with jam. Mothers made all sorts of leftovers into school lunches. A plain baked potato might be in a lunch bucket or sometimes baked bean sandwiches, with mashed baked beans between slices of bread. Boiled eggs were a favorite lunch item, and sometimes mothers packed carrots and apples. Usually students drank water with their lunches. Unlike children today, nobody had a peanut butter sandwich because peanut butter hadn't been invented yet.

If a student's mother had found time to do a

little extra baking, there might be cookies in a lunch box—usually something simple like sugar or oatmeal cookies. Chocolate was much too expensive for everyday use, so cookies were usually flavored with vanilla, nutmeg, or cinnamon instead. If the teacher planned a special treat, she might make hot chocolate out of cocoa and milk for everyone, warming it on top of the stove that sat in the middle of the room and heated the school. Then the room smelled like chocolate all afternoon.

After lunch and recess, the youngest children often studied reading and math again, while older students studied subjects such as history, geography, and nature. Boys and girls studied reading at their desks and came to the front of the room to recite for the teacher what they had learned. They usually did math exercises at the blackboard and often spelled their words on the board too. Sometimes the whole class came together to study for a subject like reading or spelling. At other times, the teacher was busy teaching many different students in many different grades. Because the teacher had so much to do with so many students in so many different grades, older children helped teach younger children their lessons. In this way, students relied on their classmates to help them learn. Classrooms could be very noisy places, with students studying and reciting many different subjects all at once. Some students learned just by listening to

Iowa students and teacher in front of school, 1886. The girls wore aprons over their dresses to help them stay clean, and almost all students went to school barefoot. *Courtesy of the State Historical Society of Iowa, Iowa City, Iowa.*

the older students recite their lessons. After a time of study, there was usually another recess in the middle of the afternoon.

Students who misbehaved in school, or who had not learned their lessons, were punished by the teacher. Those who did not learn their lessons had to stay inside and study during recess. A student who misspelled too many words in spelling class might have to stand at the front of the room and write the words correctly over and over on the blackboard, maybe one hundred times! A student who had talked instead of being quiet might have to stand in the corner or even stand at the blackboard with his or her nose touching the board. Sometimes teachers made students memorize long, boring speeches or poems as punishment. And when a student really misbehaved, he or she could be spanked or hit by the teacher. Often, teachers smacked students across the knuckles with a ruler for punishment. When the misbehaving students got home after school, they might be spanked again by their parents since parents expected their children to be good and obey the teacher while at school.

Even so, school was usually more about fun than about punishment. Today, students have plenty of places to climb and play on the playground with the swings, slides, jungle gyms, climbing walls, and basketball courts. Playgrounds were much simpler in 1900. When the students ran out to play at recess, they found a big open field that was very muddy when it rained or snowed. There might be a few swings or maybe a slide, but most of the time there was not. If students wanted to play baseball at lunch, they had to bring their own bats, gloves, and balls. More often, children played games using their imaginations.

The biggest reason that children liked to go to school was that it was a time when they always had time to play. At home, work came first. At school, though, play was on the schedule every day. With a morning and afternoon recess and a recess at lunch time, children played all sorts of games during these breaks. When the winters were cold and there was a pond or a hill nearby, students skated or went sledding during lunch. In their games they chased and caught each other, playing hide-and-seek and Fox-and-Geese. Students played Fox-and-Geese this way: "When it snowed children played Fox-and-Geese by making a circle in the snow with spokes and a center. The children chose a leader who tried to tag the children as they all ran around the circle. The last one tagged got to be the new leader."[7]

Students also played other games like marbles, a game where players drew a circle in the dirt and attempted to knock another's marble out of the ring. Sometimes children played "for keeps" and collected all of the marbles they had knocked out of the ring, but sometimes they played just for fun. Another playground game was Duck-on-a-Rock. One player placed a small rock, the duck, on top of a larger rock while the others threw their own rocks, attempting to knock the duck off of the rock.[8]

Sometimes students just played "let's pretend,"

building forts and playhouses. Lucy van Voorhis grew up in Iowa and wrote in her diary about the fun that she had at school. On one spring day, the girls spent their noon recess playing by a creek. Lucy wrote, "Today noon we went down to the branch and played 'old witch' under the bridge." Later that week, she and her friends stayed inside for recess. "At noon, we made puzzles & gave them to the others to solve." Other days, the girls told stories. On another day in June she wrote, "At noon Abbie and I made a play-house in the avenue, while some of the others made one in and on top of the coal-house . . . I have had my lessons well today and we have all had a good time." After school, the girls went to play in the creek.[9] For Lucy and her friends, fun was something they invented. Building playhouses and using their imaginations helped them have fun at recess even though their school and playground were very plain.

On Friday afternoons, teachers planned special events for the students. On those days, students learned by competing instead of sitting at their desks and studying. Sometimes boys and girls memorized poems and speeches and recited them for each other. Sometimes there were math competitions at the blackboard with everyone doing problems. The teacher started with simple problems, such as 2 + 2, and then asked harder and harder questions. When a student made an incorrect answer, he or she had to sit down. The last student left standing won. Friday afternoons were also the time for spelling bees. Again, the teacher began by asking easy questions, like how to spell "cat." As the words became harder and harder, students began to make mistakes, and they had to sit down if they could not spell a word. The last student to spell the most difficult word won the spelling bee. If it was a very special afternoon, students from another school might come to visit and join in the competition. The school with the best math student or the best speller won the day's contest.

School was also a place for special events, like celebrations of Halloween, Christmas, and the last day of school. For these celebrations, the students invited their parents and neighbors to come to the schoolhouse and join them. Seventy people went to a gathering at Hazel Hampson's school in Nebraska. Students presented poems and speeches, and afterwards there were math and spelling contests. Hazel wrote, "When we got home we were tired, but we had a good time anyway."[10]

At Halloween, the students might have a party. One country school had a carnival to raise money and students raised more than $20:

> The lanterns were all lighted and big pumpkins were placed all around the room. After the

> program the girls passed napkins to those who wanted oyster soup. We all put on our serving things and helped with the soup, for we had a large crowd. The ghosts sold popcorn and candy. The witches sold fortunes at a table and two of the girls had them guess the number of grains of corn in a bottle. A box of candy was given as a prize to the one who guessed the nearest. We could have sold more popcorn and candy than we had.[11]

Getting dressed up and going trick-or-treating was not a part of Halloween for farm children since families lived a long distance from each other and it was very difficult to go from house to house. Only children who lived in town could trick-or-treat, so farm children celebrated with school parties.

Christmas was an exciting time too. Schools hosted programs of singing and plays and served special meals. Singing was always an important part of Christmas parties, and students sang Christmas carols and other songs like "Jingle Bells." Students decorated Christmas trees, and the teacher usually gave the children small presents, like a pencil or an orange. Sometimes Santa Claus visited. When Christina Sladek went to her school's Christmas party, there was a small present for everyone. "When Santa Claus came out he went through the fireplace and turned back to the pumpkin and took a box of candy out of the pumpkin and said, 'Here is something the fairy left,' and then gave everybody a sack of candy."[12] Children thought that candy, oranges, apples, and nuts were special because they only got to eat them once or twice a year.

The last day of school was also the time for a big party. The students invited their parents to hear what they had learned. Hermann Benke was a sixteen-year-old schoolteacher when he wrote in his diary about the events he planned for the last day of school. "By the most strenuous exertion I arrange a programme and make the occasion a festival . . . On programme we have 50 exercises of a various nature including one song."[13] The program included poems, songs, and lessons, and the students showed their parents what they had learned. In addition to the program, there was food. Hermann gave his students candy, nuts, and apples, and he also gave prizes like new pencils and erasers to the students who were the best at spelling, math, and other subjects. The end of the school year was a very exciting time, and everyone for miles around came for the program and to join the celebration.

Even though most farm children left school when they turned fourteen, a very small number went on to high school or on to college, and some of them, like William Owens, became schoolteachers. To be a teacher, a boy or girl had to be sixteen years old and a graduate of the eighth grade, and then he or she had to pass a basic test. Many teachers in rural schools were female and very young, barely older than the boys and girls who were in their classes. Most had not gone to high school or college, and they had learned to teach as they watched their own teachers. Schoolteachers usually earned between $25 and $50 a month, and for this salary they had to be the teacher, the janitor, the school nurse, and the principal.

Not only were teachers important to their students, but they were very important to their own families. Being a sixteen- or seventeen-year-old teacher could be scary when facing a classroom for the first time. Rhoda Emery grew up in Minnesota, and when she was seventeen, she became a teacher, working to help her parents pay their bills. They lived on a small farm and needed the money she earned to keep the family fed and clothed. Rhoda's life as a schoolteacher was very busy. During the week, she lived away from home and taught in a country school. On the weekends, holidays, and during the summer, she went home and helped her parents on the farm. Basically, she had two jobs—one as a teacher and one as her parents' helper. She was able to use some of the money she earned to buy things that she wanted, such as books. Most of her money, though, went to her family.[14]

Rhoda wrote in her diary about the work she did as a country schoolteacher. On her very first day of work Rhoda wrote, "The first day of school is over and I for one am not sorry. I got along very well; had fifteen scholars. . . . I am awful tired. It is not so much fun as it might be." For the very first time, Rhoda was living away from home and working. Teaching school was much harder than she thought it would be. Near the end of the first week, she wrote in her diary, "Only one more day. I feel as lame as an old plough-horse tonight. My back has ached all day and I have been dreadfully cross. . . . I don't know as I shall ever like school-teaching." Over time, things became easier. She wrote, "I have prospered in school, though. I believe I have really made some improvement in the scholars in these two weeks. They have better lessons than they did at first anyway. It hardly seems possible that to-morrow is Friday. I wonder if time passes as quickly with the pupils as it does with me."[15] Rhoda began teaching when she was seventeen and was a teacher and school principal all her life.

Teachers were very important. Good teachers helped their students learn new skills and new information that helped them improve their lives as farmers or as anything else they wanted to be. Teachers were also role models. Often teachers were farm boys and farm girls who had grown up in the very same community, had gone to school with some of their students, and were an example of what a boy or girl could do if he or she studied hard and learned their lessons well. Teachers often "boarded around," actually living with the families of the students they taught. In this way they were a part of their communities. For boys and girls who wanted to be something other than a farmer when grown, teaching was often a first steppingstone to another kind of work.

School was a big part of children's lives. One woman recalled what life was like when she was a young child and explained why she and her friends liked to go to school. "In those days they didn't have any TV. They didn't have any ball games to go to, or anything. They just went home and went to work. Changed their school clothes, hung them up behind the door, and went to work—feeding horses or cattle or chickens—maybe even chopping cotton or picking cotton after school. . . . School was really a vacation to them, as much as anything else."[16]

Schools gave children the opportunity to learn, to study, and to play. A good education gave them opportunities, whether a boy or girl decided to be a successful farmer or to leave the farm for another kind of work. Going to school meant that a boy or girl had choices about what to do with his or her life.

4
PLAYING ON THE FARM
Farm Children Making Fun for Themselves

Finding the Fun in Everyday Life

Sarah Gillespie of Iowa[1]

Sarah Gillespie grew up on a farm near Manchester, Iowa. When she was just eleven years old, she began keeping a diary, writing in it the story of her day-to-day life. Like most farm girls her age, her most important job was to help her parents with chores. In May of 1879 she wrote in her diary, "help ma all day am tired."[2]

One of Sarah's favorite activities was writing in her diary. Every year at Christmas, she received a new diary. Writing in it gave her the opportunity to think about the day she just had and what she might like to do the next. In the beginning, her spelling and her punctuation weren't very good, but in time she learned how to write well. She liked writing in her diary so much that she kept a journal from the time she was eleven until she was nearly ninety years old.

Sarah was a busy girl who had lots of fun with her family, neighbors, and friends. She liked all sorts of activities and games like playing ball or going wading in the creek with her brother. Sarah also liked to sew quilts and embroider, and she entered her best efforts in the competition at the county fair. In the winter, she liked to go sledding.

When Sarah's family and their neighbors had parties, they usually invited everyone. Parties weren't just for boys and girls or for their parents, but for whole families, and everyone came together for neighborhood events. When some neighbors of the Gillespies had a wedding anniversary, everyone came to celebrate, bringing the couple presents. Sarah wrote in her diary about the event. "We had them married over again. We had a splendid good time."[3] At the anniversary party, besides the "pretend" wedding ceremony, there was lots of food. "We had supper all kinds of cake pie & best of all water melons & musk melons. they presented ma & pa with a set of glass dishes a real nice time we had."[4]

Practically every month, Sarah and her family went to a party—a birthday party, an anniversary, or some other excuse to celebrate. One night, the family was getting ready to go to bed when there was a knock at the door. Six wagonloads of visitors had arrived for a surprise party! There wasn't any special event at all—people just wanted to have some fun. They all played games, ate candy, and popped popcorn. The visitors stayed until after three o'clock in the morning, and Sarah wrote in her journal, "hope they will come again."[5]

Farm families usually lived a long way from their neighbors, and they might not be able to see each other every day or even every week. What's more, in the days before farm families owned telephones, it was not even possible for friends and neighbors to talk with each other without being face to face. People had to visit each other to be able to talk. Families like Sarah's also liked to go to church and to events at the school because they then had the chance to see other families and visit with them. Most of the time, though, families only traveled a few miles from home. They needed to be able to get home at the end of the day to feed and milk cows and take care of the other animals on the farm. So leaving the farm for more than a day was something families rarely did.

Holidays such as Christmas were also a time

for fun both at school and at home, but not quite in the same way as today. Sarah's parents gave her presents, but those presents were fewer in number and less expensive than what children ask for today. One Christmas, her family decorated a very small tree that they made from a limb of a plum tree, and they hung their presents on it. Sarah received a small, embroidered picture and a pair of slippers.[6] The next year, she received "a Cocoanut, China candle stick, wax candle (red) A yard of Ribbon & some crackers," and she wrote, "Santa Claus was very good this time."[7] Sarah and her family usually could not afford luxuries, so getting a ribbon or a new diary or a pair of slippers was a special event. Along with a Christmas tree, there might be food such as a turkey and stuffing or pie. Sometimes children received something unusual to eat, like an orange, a banana, or a coconut. It didn't take much to make a Christmas extraordinary.

Sarah Gillespie did not own expensive games and toys. Instead she turned the farm into her playground and made do with the few homemade toys she owned. Just writing in her journal or sewing on her quilt was a favorite activity. The most important way she had fun was by spending time with family, friends, and neighbors. Because they didn't have the money to "buy" their fun, they made it themselves, and being with friends was and still is the best way to do that.

As Sarah's story shows, growing up on a farm meant that children played differently from children today. Since most farm children's time was taken up with work and school, they had less play time. Parents only allowed play time when all of the chores were done. Since farm families rarely had money to spend on anything that wasn't absolutely necessary, most of the children's toys were homemade.

Farm families rarely had money to spend on toys at the country store. When farm children walked into a store in town, they saw barrels full of nails, bins full of boards, and shovels hanging on the walls. They smelled vinegar in barrels and licorice in jars on the counter. Because stores sold so many different things, they had only a small number of toys. Instead children looked in the Sears, Roebuck or Montgomery Wards catalogs, which arrived usually around Christmastime, to find the toys they liked the best. Boys and girls were excited to see page after page of toys and to imagine the games they could play with a new bicycle or a

Iowa girls and their toys, ca. 1905. The older girl has a store-bought doll while the younger is using corn cobs like Lincoln Logs. *W. A. Warren Collection. Courtesy of the State Historical Society of Iowa, Iowa City, Iowa.*

bat and glove. Because children looked at the pictures and wished for toys and games, they called the Sears, Roebuck catalog the "wish book."

Most children only had one or two store-bought toys. Girls might own a special doll or two made out of china, wax, or bisque, which is unglazed pottery that is hard like china but not shiny. Children sometimes received a toy stove, a bicycle, or some other toy that could not be made at home. Boys might have a few store-bought toys such as mechanical cars, toy cannons, marbles, a steamship or a steam engine. Some families bought or made chessboards, checkerboards, or backgammon sets so everyone could play a game together. Christmas time was usually the only time of year when parents bought toys.

More often, though, children or their parents turned common household items into toys or made toys by hand. Chipped cups and plates and worn-out pots and pans from her mother's kitchen became a girl's toy dishes. Old crates and boxes could easily become cupboards for a play kitchen or a bed for a doll. Boys and girls could use an old wagon for "let's pretend" trips to town and far distant lands. Parents and children built many toys as well, such as wagons and sleds. One boy made a hand-cranked tractor out of an apple peeler. He clamped the apple peeler "to a short piece of board with skate wheels nailed to its ends," and commented,

"My! how it clawed at the dirt to gain tractive power as I turned the crank at the top."[8] Even though his machine did not look exactly like a tractor, it moved like one, and he was proud of his invention. Another boy made a doll bed for his younger sister, Agnes Mary. She had seen a beautiful doll bed in a store, but her parents had no money to buy toys, so instead her brother made one for her out of a crate. Agnes Mary wrote, "I watched him carefully separating the boards on the crate, making a smooth, sturdy bed and painting it blue gray; a bed that far surpassed the smaller, fragile one I had seen in the store. I was delighted! It was mine! Made for me! I treasured it for years."[9] Her brother had the fun of making the bed while Agnes Mary had the fun of playing with it.

Although girls treasured beautiful store-bought dolls with china, wax, or bisque heads, they also loved their homemade dolls. A doll could be made out of almost anything. Mothers sewed dolls out of scraps of fabric, made them out of corn husks, and even used corn cobs for dolls. The girls enjoyed helping make the doll, deciding what it should look like, and sewing clothes for it. Girls also played with paper dolls cut from scrap paper and decorated with ink or paint. Often girls also cut out the prettiest pictures of people in the Sears, Roebuck catalog and turned them into paper dolls.

For fun, sometimes children also liked to curl up by the stove and read in the evening when they had a little spare time. Most families owned only one or two books because, like so many things, books were expensive. Families might only have a copy of the Bible and another book or two. However, many families had the Sears, Roebuck and Montgomery Ward catalogs, and children read them just like books, looking at the pictures and imagining life in different places. Schools usually had a small collection of books that students could borrow, and some towns had libraries where children could check out books. Some of the books they read were ones that children read today, such as *Little Men*, *Little Women*, *The Adventures of Tom Sawyer*, *Black Beauty*, and *Anne of Green Gables*. Children also read magazines and newspapers written just for them. Instead of reading *Scholastic* or *Highlights*, children read the *Youth's Companion* and *Saint Nicholas Magazine*.

A few newspapers published for grown-ups included special pages written just for children. Boys and girls particularly liked how the newspapers included letters written by other children from across the United States. Children wrote to the papers about their families, their schools, their pets, and the work they did, and they saw their letters published. Some letters described farm life and the many activities children enjoyed, and one of those letters was from ten-year-old Nebraskan Freda Mae Rockefeller. In her letter to a newspaper, Freda wrote, "We are twenty-six miles from a railroad station, and fuel is scarce here. . . . I am the only child and get very lonesome; no amusements; no school and no church to go to, nor any books to read. I am very fond of reading. A neighbor's little girl loaned me her Sunday School papers which I read over and over." Many other children read Freda's letter, wanted to help, and sent her "many letters, papers, and books" to help keep her from being lonesome.[10]

Helena Karella, who also grew up in Nebraska, wrote to the newspaper to explain why she thought living on a farm was better than living in a city. "The spring has said goodbye and beautiful summer is here. The birds, bees, and ants are always busy. So are the happy boys and girls that live on a farm. They always have plenty to do and always have plenty of time for play. I would lots rather live on a farm than in a city, for on a farm you can skate in winter and pick flowers in summer and always have a good time."[11] Letters from the children allowed boys and girls across the country to understand what life was like on farms in different places.

Pets were an important part of children's lives too. Farm children had pet cats, dogs, and rabbits,

Minnesota boy and his goat cart, ca. 1900. *Photograph by Harry D. Ayer. #SA3.9/r4. Courtesy of the Minnesota Historical Society, St. Paul, Minnesota.*

but they also had other pets like horses they particularly liked. Parents might give a boy or a girl a colt to raise and train. Although full-grown horses generally worked in the fields, plowing or doing other chores, when the horses weren't working, boys and girls had the opportunity to go for a ride, exploring the land around their farms.

Children trained other working animals too. Some boys trained calves that grew to be mighty oxen capable of pulling the heaviest loads on the farm. Other children had pet goats, and the goats could pull a small cart and give a boy or a girl a ride. Alice Brackett, who lived on a Nebraska farm, began feeding some pet lambs when they were newborns. By the time they were about six months old, though, she wasn't able to keep them any longer. "They chewed the nipples on the bottles and I had to stop feeding them. They soon grew large and were put in the lot with the other sheep."[12] Although children treated some animals as pets, often having a farm animal for a pet meant that a boy or girl had to give it up as it grew too big or at some point became part of the family's meal.

Animals worked on the farm, and farm families rarely wasted food on an animal that didn't have a purpose. Even dogs and cats had a purpose since dogs could herd sheep or protect the family, and cats hunted and killed mice and rats. Walter Morgan, who lived in Shiloh Hills, Illinois, described his dog and its work around the farm. "I have a shepherd dog named Tony, which was brought from Missouri and given to me by one of my uncles last fall. She helps me drive the cows from the pasture every evening. She catches a great many mice."[13]

Even without pets, children always enjoyed the outdoors. Most farmhouses were small, noisy, and busy places, so mothers sent their children outside to play, giving them many opportunities to explore the land around them. In the summer, children swam and waded in ponds, streams, and lakes, and they made collections of interesting rocks, insects, and flowers. They looked for frogs and went fishing. They picked berries in the woods and took them home for their mothers to make into pies and jam. Children climbed trees, sat high in their branches, and built playhouses out of trees and stumps. If a child was out early in the morning or later in the evening, he or she might see possums, raccoons, and deer, animals that normally came out at night. Sometimes children simply enjoyed lying in the grass under a tree, watching the birds and insects fly by or shutting their eyes and listening to all of the different noises of summer.

Olive Everts, who was ten years old, described the fun things she did in a letter to a children's paper: "We are having vacation now, in our school.

My little sister and I enjoy ourselves very much. Sometimes we go to the grove and hear the little birds sing and watch the little fish swim in the creek, and the squirrels, as they play around; and sometimes we go down to the hay field and watch the men put up hay, which we think is nice fun; and then again Ma makes us stay in the house and wipe dishes, and do chores, which we think is not quite so funny. Every night I take a ride if I like. It seems that we enjoy ourselves more than the little children that live in town."[14]

Children also played in all of the different buildings on the farm. Barns were places to explore since there were often nests of new kittens to be found, calves and colts to visit, and favorite animals to feed and pet. The loft of the barn, filled with hay, was a good place to sit and daydream on a rainy day and a very good place to play hide-and-seek. If parents allowed it (it was a little bit dangerous!), boys and girls could have a swing in the barn that took them high up into the air, almost into the rafters, much higher than any swing at a playground. Then they could jump from the swing into the deep, soft hay.

Wintertime created many other ways to enjoy playing outdoors. Children went sliding on the ice on lakes and ponds. Sometimes they had skates, but often they just slid using their everyday shoes.

Kansas children in a snowy yard between 1905 and 1915. Children played in the snow and built forts and snowmen. *Everett M. Wentworth Collection. *128. Courtesy of the State Historical Society of Kansas, Topeka, Kansas.*

If they lived someplace cold enough for snow, they made snowmen, had snowball fights, built snow forts, and lay down in the snow to make snow angels. They slid down hills on sleds and toboggans, and if there were no hills, they hitched their sleds behind a horse or another animal and went for a ride. Josephine Beyer, who grew up in Nebraska, played with her brother on the ice and the snow. She wrote, "I was down skating . . . My brother Johnie has a sled and a dog. He hitches him on the sled and hauls me on the ice. We have lots of fun."[15]

Children enjoyed a variety of activities. In the winter, some boys trapped animals such as rabbits, mink, and foxes. The children had fun outside, but trapping was also work since the boys sold the furs for money. One boy wrote a letter to the children's page of the *Nebraska Farmer*, explaining that he had gotten traps from his aunt and that in the first week of trapping he had earned $2.40.[16] While $2.40 does not seem like much money today, it was a lot back then. Books cost as little as fifty cents, and a chocolate bar cost a nickel. Another boy earned $30 in a month of trapping.[17] Fishing and hunting could also be both work and play since the animals the boys hunted or the fish they caught also became food for the family.

Lots of girls also enjoyed cooking. When Verna Kylander was ten years old, she decided to bake her very first pie. "One time my mother and father went to town and left my little sister and me at home . . . They left at eight o'clock and had ten miles to go to town. We girls played house for a while and then we thought we would surprise our mother by baking an apple pie . . . When it had baked we took it out and let it cool. As soon as it cooled we put it in the lower part of the cupboard. This was our first pie. Mamma and papa were sure surprised when they came home. We had lots of fun that day."[18] Even though cooking was work, girls liked to bake pies and cakes and make candy.

As mentioned earlier, farm children turned some of their work into play to keep themselves interested while they did chores. One boy's job was to herd the cows along with his brothers. He wrote, "This spring we had to herd cows. We had lots of fun too. We have an old cow that I like to ride. When I first got on her she ran a long ways, and I tried to round up the cows but I could not do it. We have another old cow that I tried to ride, but my brother twisted her tail and she pitched me off. It made me mad. I am eleven years old, but I like to ride cows."[19] Although this boy liked to ride cows, riding made the cows tired, and playing around large animals such as cows, horses, and pigs was often dangerous.

Children also enjoyed events away from home such as circuses, fairs, and parties. Circuses traveled by train, and everyone was excited when the circus came to the area. If boys and girls were lucky, they went to town to watch the circus train arrive. Standing next to the track when the train arrived, boys and girls saw all sorts of animals they had never seen before, such as elephants, monkeys, lions, and tigers. They saw clowns, jugglers, and tightrope walkers. Sometimes boys and girls went home afterward and pretended they had a circus in their own yard, building tents out of quilts and decorating the family's wagon and horses like a circus wagon.

The fair was also an exciting event, especially when combined with a trip to town. In 1913, Matilda Kramer described her family's journey to the county fair. Just getting to town took four and a half hours. "My sister, brother and I went to the county fair this year . . . We ate our dinner and went out to the fair grounds where we saw lots of fruit, vegetables, poultry, hogs, cattle, and sheep, and also a trotting horse race. We rode in the merry-go-round at the fair grounds and then we went back to town. We saw two moving picture shows and surely had a fine time."[20] Going to the movies, or the moving pictures, as Matilda called them, was a big event. In 1913, most farm boys and girls had never seen a movie, but Matilda and her brother and sister were able to see two.

Another exciting time was the Fourth of July. Communities celebrated American Independence Day with picnics, speeches, contests, and fireworks. When a family went to a celebration in town, they found lemonade and ice cream to buy, those special treats children seldom ate. If a family stayed at their home for the day, they had a picnic or some other special holiday meal. The Fourth of July was a big summer celebration, a chance for a welcome break from work and a visit with friends and family.

One of the biggest differences between playing now and playing then was the freedom and responsibility that boys and girls had. Today, children often play close to home with their parents watching them. Many years ago, children often played out of their parents' sight without any grown-ups watching them at all. Parents were busy with their own work and did not always have time to watch their children. A farm was big, and mothers were often at work in the house or garden and fathers in the barn or fields. Because their parents were not always watching, children watched out for each other and took care of their brothers, sisters, and friends.

One hundred years ago, work and school kept boys and girls very busy, but they made time for play too. They had toys and games, played with animals, and found ways to turn work into play. Holidays were filled with fun, and if children were really lucky, they went to the circus or the fair. Even though living and working on a farm, boys and girls could have lots of fun.

CONCLUSION

How Things Changed and Why

Growing Up and Making Choices

The Ise Children of Kansas[1]

Between the 1870s and the 1890s, twelve children were born on the Ise family farm in Osborne County, Kansas. Although the oldest boy, Henry Albert, died as a baby, all of the other brothers and sisters lived to be adults.

Theirs was a large and busy family. Like other farm children, the Ise brothers and sisters did lots of work. All of the children worked in the garden and the fields. Like Rose Wilder and her family, they even picked dandelion leaves that their mother made into salad for dinner. One of the jobs the Ise children liked the least was picking potato bugs off the plants so the bugs would not eat the potatoes. The older girls were busy helping their mother, Rosa, take care of their little brothers and sisters. In fact, when the oldest girl, Alma, was only four years old, it was her job to take care of her younger brother and sister. Edward was two, and Minnie was a baby! Even with eleven children to divide the chores, there was plenty of work to keep everyone busy. The children's help was particularly important because their father, Henry, was often ill and unable to work. In fact, he died in 1900, when his youngest child, Frank, was only five years old.

The most important influence in the Ise children's lives, however, was education. Their mother grew up in a very poor family and only attended school once, for a single half day, then had to go home to take care of her brothers and sisters. So when her own children were old enough to go to school, she wanted them to have something she missed—a good education. Even though the Ise children sometimes missed school to help at home, they attended class as much as they could for as many years as they could. All of the children went to grade school and high school. As mentioned earlier, very few young people went to college then, but nine of the eleven Ise children did. In fact, five of them went beyond college, attending graduate school or law school, eventually becoming teachers, lawyers, a pharmacist, and an optometrist. Only one child, Edward, grew up to be a farmer.

For one of the Ise children, John, education was particularly important, and he grew up to be a college professor and writer. As a child, he was ill with polio. (Because there are now shots that protect people from polio, very few children get the disease today). Polio paralyzed John's legs, and he could not work like his brothers and sisters. While the other children worked in the fields, he stayed around the house and helped his mother. John's parents knew he could never be a farmer because he could not use his legs to walk, run, or do chores, so they made other plans for John's life, giving him the opportunity to study as much as he could. Going to school and having an education meant that John could support himself by using his brain rather than his body. When he grew up, John Ise became an economics professor at the University of Kansas, and he wrote many books, including one called *Sod and Stubble*, a book telling the story of his family's life in Kansas.

Education gave the Ise children wonderful opportunities. By staying in school and studying, the Ise brothers and sisters were able to choose what they wanted to be, whether a farmer, a teacher, a lawyer, or a pharmacist. These children never again had to work in the fields or pick bugs off of the potatoes unless they wanted to.

In 1900 and even in the 1920s and 1930s, most farm children worked on their farms like the Ise children. For most, work came first. Unlike the Ise children, most quit school to work on their parents' farms before they ever had the chance to go to high school. For most farm children, even the Ise children, their help was absolutely essential to their families' survival, and families managed because everyone contributed.

Some farm children, as they grew up, were happy with the farm and with the kind of life they lived. They enjoyed working outside and spending time with animals such as horses and cows. They learned to be responsible, imaginative, and hardworking. Although many farm children loved to work and play outdoors, life on the farm could be difficult. Farm children worked outside in every kind of weather, from the blazing hot summer sun to the freezing cold winter wind. The children worked more than they played or studied, and they often sacrificed time from school and play to tend to the needs of their parents' farms.

Other boys and girls were less happy because of the hard work or because of the isolation of farm life keeping them away from town and their friends. These children often decided to make lives for themselves off the farm when given a chance. Some chose to go on to high school and college or to move to the small towns and cities, wanting to raise their own children in a different kind of place. As cities grew and the United States changed, young people had more and more opportunities to leave the farm. In the cities, they worked in schools, factories, and other places of business. Especially with a good education, young people could choose many different jobs.

The uncertainty of farm life was hard to accept because farming was a difficult way to make a living. Although farmers planted seeds for crops, much could go wrong between planting and harvesting. The weather could bring too much rain or too little, or hail and wind could flatten growing wheat, corn, and oats. Horses, cows, and chickens could get sick and die. Even with all of the farmers' hard work, they had no guarantee their work would pay off. Often farm children, when they grew up, chose to avoid the uncertainty of life on a farm.

In 1776, at the time of the American Revolution, ninety out of every one hundred Americans lived on a farm. Because nearly all farm work had to be done by hand, growing crops to feed the nation's people took an enormous amount of work. Even in 1900, most farm work was still done by hand, and most American families lived on farms or in small towns. But as the years went by, fewer and fewer people lived on farms. By the 1950s, times had changed. Most farm children lived in houses with electric lights and central heating. Some families still had chickens to feed and cows to milk, but that was less and less often the case. There was also less work for children to do in the morning before school, and then the school bus came to take the children to school. At the end of the day, boys and girls went to after-school activities, and there was more time to play and more time to rest. In these ways, life on the farm had become easier and more comfortable.

Today, fewer than two out of every one hundred Americans live on farms, so most children live in suburbs and large towns. Farm machines now do much of the work that people once did. Since machines can do the work of many people, it is no longer necessary for so many people to live on farms. Inventions such as tractors and combines, which do the work horses once did, help farmers work much more quickly and easily.

Farms are also bigger today than they used to be, and farm homes are different from those in the past. Although electricity, telephones, and running water came to farms more slowly than to cities, by the 1950s, most farms had these new technologies. Farm families today have radios, televisions, and computers, just like people in the cities and suburbs. With all these changes, farm life is far different now than it was in the past.

Although children who live on farms today may have lives a bit different from children in cities and suburbs, their lives are more like those of children in towns than those of children who lived on farms one hundred years ago. Farm children go to school, play with their friends, use computers and cell phones, and ride in cars, just like children in town.

Many of the difficulties of being a farm child disappeared with time. But perhaps some of the good things about farm living have disappeared too. As times changed, children spent fewer hours working with their parents, and children did less for themselves. They also spent less time enjoying the outdoors, and they were less important to the family's survival on the farm. Over time, children's lives have become more and more alike, no matter where they live. Only you can imagine how you would have enjoyed living in that other world, a world of a farm child one hundred years ago.

NOTES

INTRODUCTION

1. "Young People," *Nebraska Farmer*, February 7, 1912, 161.
2. Ibid., December 17, 1913, 1181.
3. Ibid., February 28, 1912, 257.

CHAPTER 1

1. For more stories about the Wilder family, and especially stories written by Rose Wilder Lane, see William T. Anderson, editor, *A Little House Sampler* (New York: Harper and Row, 1988).
2. Rose Wilder Lane, "Grandpa's Fiddle," in Anderson, 70–86.
3. Lane, "The Ozark Years," in Anderson, 88–96.
4. William A. Owens, *This Stubborn Soil* (New York: Charles Scribner's Sons, 1966), 144.
5. Anyone who wants to try cooking nineteenth-century reci-

pes should see Barbara M. Walker, *The Little House Cookbook: Frontier Foods from Laura Ingalls Wilder's Classic Stories* (New York: HarperCollins Publishers, 1979). She provides recipes for such nineteenth-century staples as fried salt pork, bean soup, and pulled candy (taffy).
6. J. C. Witter, *Pioneer Children* (Newton: Mennonite Press, 1985), 58.
7. Henry Wylie Norton diary, February 18, 1885, in C. Robert Haywood and Sandra Jarvis, *"A Funnie Place, No Fences": Teenagers' Views of Kansas, 1867–1900* (Lawrence: Division of Continuing Education, University of Kansas, 1992), 122.

CHAPTER 2

1. For the story of Ralph Moody, see Ralph Moody, *Little Britches* (New York: Norton, 1950), *Man of the Family* (New York: Norton, 1951), and *Mary Emma and Company* (New York: Norton, 1961).
2. *Little Britches,* 13.
3. Ibid., 69.
4. Ibid., 171–172.
5. For good general discussions of farm children and work, see John Ise, *Sod and Stubble: The Story of a Kansas Farm* (Lawrence: University Press of Kansas, 1996); Elliott West, *Growing Up with the Country: Childhood on the Farm Western Frontier* (Albuquerque: University of New Mexico Press, 1898), 73–100; Pamela Riney-Kehrberg, *Childhood on the Farm: Work, Play and Coming of Age in the Midwest* (Lawrence: University Press of Kansas, 2005), 36–60.
6. John Talcott Norton diary, May 8, 1879, in Haywood and Jarvis, 113.
7. Mammie Eberle diary in Haywood and Jarvis, 142–143.
8. Riney-Kehrberg, 54.

9. Mammie Eberle diary, October 1874, in Haywood and Jarvis, 132.
10. Ibid., March 10, 1874, in Haywood and Jarvis, 136.
11. Ibid., June 24, 1875, in Haywood and Jarvis, 146.
12. Riney-Kehrberg, 44–45.
13. Interview with Elsie Swafford Riney by author, June 1989.
14. Martha Farnsworth, "'Boys!' A Girl's Diary," in Haywood and Jarvis, 299.
15. John Talcott Norton diary, January 12, 1878, in Haywood and Jarvis, 106.

CHAPTER 3

1. For the story of William A. Owens, see William A. Owens, *This Stubborn Soil* (New York: Charles Scribner's Sons, 1966).
2. Ibid., 66.
3. Ibid., 141.
4. Ibid., 205.
5. Ibid., 228.
6. Thad Sitton and Milam C. Rowold, *Ringing the Children In: Texas Country Schools* (College Station: Texas A&M University Press, 1987), 25.
7. Shirley Mollett Webb, typescript reminiscence, "Reminiscence of School Days." Manuscripts Division, Kansas State Historical Society, Topeka, Kansas, n.p.
8. William S. Miller, *Growing Up in Goose Lake.* (William S. Miller, 1974), 20–24.
9. Quotations from the diary of Lucy van Voorhis White, Iowa Women's Archives, University of Iowa, Iowa City, Iowa, April/May 1882.
10. Hazel Hampson, "Young People," *Nebraska Farmer*, February 7, 1912, 161.

11. Mary Chappell, "Young People," *Nebraska Farmer*, December 2, 1916, 1253.
12. Christina Sladek, "Young People," *Nebraska Farmer*, January 23, 1907, 73.
13. Hermann Benke, April 21, 1866, microfilm copy of manuscript diary, Manuscripts Division, Kansas State Historical Society, Topeka, Kansas.
14. Rhoda J. Emery diary, June 18, 1894, Rhoda J. Emery and Family Papers, Manuscript Diary 1889, Manuscripts Collection, Minnesota Historical Society, St. Paul, Minnesota.
15. Ibid.
16. Quotation from Susie Bell Anderson, in Sitton and Rowold, 90.

CHAPTER 4

1. To read more of Sarah Gillespie Huftalen's diary, see Suzanne L. Bunkers, editor, *"All Will Yet Be Well": The Diary of Sarah Gillespie Huftalen, 1873–1952* (Iowa City: University of Iowa Press, 1993).
2. Ibid., 29.
3. Ibid., 19.
4. Ibid., 20.
5. Ibid., 38–39.
6. Ibid., 21.
7. Ibid., 27.
8. Maurice Minor, *Three in a Hill* (New York: Carlton Press, 1979), 121–126.
9. Agnes Mary Kolshorn, "Children's Life on the Valley Farm, 1882–1902" in Kolshorn Family History, Manuscripts Collection, Minnesota Historical Society, St. Paul, Minnesota.
10. Freda Mae Rockefeller, "Young People," *Nebraska Farmer*, February 7, 1912, 161 and June 26, 1912, 645.

11. Helena Karella, "Work and Play Club," *Nebraska Farmer,* July 3, 1907, 593.

12. Alice Esther Brackett, "Young People," *Nebraska Farmer,* April 2, 1913, 437.

13. Walter Morgan, "What Uncle Frank Says," *American Young Folks* 3, no. 9 (September 1877), 140.

14. Olive V. Everts, "Our Post Office," *American Young Folks* 5, no. 9 (September 1879), 139.

15. Josephine Beyer, "Work and Play Club," *Nebraska Farmer,* March 20, 1907, 299.

16. Roger Wilson, "Young People," *Nebraska Farmer,* March 13, 1912, 324.

17. Alvin W. McCord, "Young People," *Nebraska Farmer,* October 1, 1913, 953.

18. Verna Kylander, "Young People," *Nebraska Farmer,* March 15, 1916, 381.

19. Arthur O. Single, "Young People," *Nebraska Farmer,* June 19, 1912, 629.

20. Matilda Kramer, "Young People," *Nebraska Farmer,* October 15, 1913, 1001.

CONCLUSION

1. For the story of the Ise family, see John Ise, *Sod and Stubble: The Story of a Kansas Farm* (Lawrence: University Press of Kansas, 1996).

THEN AND NOW

Questions Worth Considering

CHAPTER 1

1. What are some of your favorite foods? Do you think that children ate your favorite foods one hundred years ago? What are some of the foods they ate? Do you help make meals at your house?
2. How were children's clothes different one hundred years ago?
3. Look at the pictures of the log house, sod house, and dugout. Why did families live in houses made of logs and dirt instead of houses made of boards and brick? What do you think it was like to live in these houses? How is this different from your home?

CHAPTER 2

1. Why did children spend so much time working? What kind of jobs did they do? How do you help your parents? What kind of work do you do around your house?
2. What kind of work was boys' work? What kind of work was girls' work? Did boys only do "boys' work" and girls only do "girls' work"?
3. How did boys and girls turn their work into play? Do you ever turn your work into play? Do you have contests with your brothers and sisters?

CHAPTER 3

1. What did schools look like one hundred years ago? How were the schools back then different from the school you attend today?
2. Why did children like to go to school?
3. What special events did students celebrate every year? How is this different from or similar to celebrations at your school?
4. What qualities did a person need to have to teach school? What was it like to be a young schoolteacher?

CHAPTER 4

1. Why did children make their own toys and use their imaginations so much? What did boys and girls use

to make toys? What kind of toys do you have today? Have you made any of your toys?

2. What kind of pets did farm children have? Do you have pets at home?
3. When boys and girls went outside to play, what did they do? Do you go outside to play? How is the way you play the same or different from the way that children played one hundred years ago? Do you think you have as much fun as they did?

CONCLUSION

1. How is life today different than life on farms long ago? Would you like to have lived on a farm in 1900? What do you think would have been fun? What do you think would have been difficult?
2. How do modern inventions (such as running water, indoor toilets, televisions, telephones, and computers) make your life easier today? Would you want to try to live without them?

VOCABULARY

Boarding around: Teachers often boarded around, meaning that they lived and ate with the families of the children they taught. Teachers often lived a week or two with one family and then moved on to live with another.

Claim shanty: A claim shanty was a small, square house made out of a single layer of boards, usually having only one or two rooms. They were very cheap and quick to build.

Combine: A combine is a machine with an engine that both cuts the crop and threshes it at harvest time. Combines are used to cut and thresh crops such as wheat, corn, and oats.

Chopping cotton: Chopping is weeding and is usually done with a hoe.

Dugout: A dugout is a house that is dug out of the ground like a cave or a basement.

Feed sacks: Farmers bought food for their animals, such as chickens, packaged in cloth feed sacks. Families used the empty sacks to make clothing, diapers, dish towels, and other household items.

Harvest: Harvest is the process of bringing the crops in from the field when they are ripe. Crops are usually harvested in the late summer and fall.

Herding: Herding is when someone watches and tends animals such as cattle while they eat. Herding also involves moving animals from one place to another, usually while the herder rides on horseback.

Locusts: Locusts are insects that like to eat plants. In the late nineteenth and early twentieth centuries, there were plagues of locusts that came and ate the crops across very large parts of the western United States. Locusts and grasshoppers look a lot alike, and people often called locusts grasshoppers.

Outhouse or privy: An outhouse or privy is an outdoor toilet consisting of a small building sitting over a pit. These were usually located in back of the farmhouse.

Plowing: Plowing is the process of making a field ready for planting. Farmers plowed with horses and later with tractors.

Profit: Profit is the money that is left over after the crops are sold and all of the expenses of growing the crop have been paid.

Quarantine: People were quarantined when they became ill with dangerous diseases. No one outside of their families could visit when a family posted a quarantine sign. In this way, people tried to keep diseases from spreading and making more people sick.

Root vegetables: Root vegetables are vegetables like carrots, potatoes, onions, parsnips, and turnips that grow largely underground. Only their leaves grow above the soil. People ate lots of root vegetables because they lasted a long time after they were harvested.

Self-sufficiency: Being self-sufficient means growing most of what a family needs to survive on its own farm.

Slate: A slate was a small piece of blackboard that students wrote on at their own desks. A slate could be erased and used over and over again. Today, students use paper instead.

Slop: Slop is a name for leftovers. Farmers fed slop to hogs.

Sod house: A sod house is a house that is made by piling two-foot-wide strips of sod (packed dirt with grass roots in it) on top of each other to make walls.

Threshing: Threshing is the process of removing grain from a stalk after it has been harvested. Wheat, which is used to make bread, is a crop that is threshed. Originally grain was threshed from the stalk by beating the stalks. Later, threshing machines were invented for this purpose.

Tractors: Tractors are farm machines with engines; these are used to pull a plow or provide the kind of power for farm tasks horses once provided.

Trapping: Trapping is the capturing and killing of wild animals, usually for their fur.

INDEX

ABOUT THE AUTHOR

Pamela Riney-Kehrberg, professor of history at Iowa State University, is also the author of the scholarly history *Childhood on the Farm: Work, Play, and Coming of Age in the Midwest.* Her interest in children's history was inspired by four grandparents who all grew up poor on Kansas farms.